PAPER TIGERS

STORIES OF
IRISH
NEWSPAPERS
BY THE PEOPLE
WHO MAKE
THEM

HUGH ORAM

APPLETREE PRESS
in association with

For Bernadette

Published by
The Appletree Press Ltd
19-21 Alfred Street
Belfast BT2 8DL
in association with RTE
1993

Copyright © Hugh Oram and the contributors, 1993

All rights reserved. No part of this publication
may be reproduced or transmitted in any form
or by any means, electronic or mechanical,
photocopying, recording or in any information
or retrieval system, without prior permission
in writing from the publisher.

British Library Cataloguing-in-Publication Data
A catalogue record for this book is
available from the British Library.

ISBN 0 86281 439 1

9 8 7 6 5 4 3 2 1

PAPER TIGERS

Contents

	Acknowledgements	*7*
	Introduction	*9*
1	Characters of the Dublin Newspaper Trade	*11*
2	Vincent Gill and the Longford News	*20*
3	The Sunday World	*27*
4	The Kilkenny People and the Kildare Nationalist	*33*
5	The Irish Times in the 1960s	*42*
6	The Skibbereen Eagle and the Southern Star	*53*
7	Hot Metal Technology	*60*
8	Belfast's Papers in the Early 1970s	*67*
9	The Gossip Columnists	*77*
10	Smokey Joe and the Munster Express	*84*
11	The Sunday Newspapers	*92*
12	The Cork Examiner	*99*
13	The Derry Papers	*105*
14	The Meath and Louth Papers	*126*
15	The Evening Press	*124*
16	The Mayo Papers	*130*
17	The Critics	*137*

Acknowledgements

I SHOULD LIKE TO THANK my wife Bernadette for her unending patience and understanding twice over for *Paper Tigers*, once for the radio series and again for the book.

I would like to express my appreciation to Michael Littleton, RTE Radio head of features, who took up the idea of a series on Irish newspapers and enabled it to be developed in radio format. My producer for the series, Dick Warner, maintained an air of imperturbable calm throughout the proceedings, while I would also like to thank the equally dedicated RTE sound engineers and Peter Doyle and Ian Lee in RTE Sound Archives. Paddy Clarke in RTE's public affairs department contributed much to the series's success in terms of media publicity.

Douglas Gageby, former editor of *The Irish Times*, gave an immense amount of help and encouragement not only during the production of the radio series, but during the preparation of this book.

I should also like to thank the many people in the newspaper industry who took part in the series and whose comments are recorded in the book. Many subsequently helped with the production of the book by supplying appropriate photographs. I want to express my appreciation to all the library staff at *The Irish Times*, including John Gibson and Tony Lennon, for their help from the photographic archives, Jim Cooke, *Irish Times* production director, Gerry Mulvey, formerly of *The Irish Times*, Pat Keegan of the *Irish Press* group, Jim Griffiths and Tom McCann of the *Irish Press* library, John J. Finegan, former drama critic, *Evening Herald*, and Sean Galavan, Irish Print Union.

Other personalities and newspapers who gave invaluable photographic assistance were Derek Cobbe (Longford); the *Cork Examiner* (Tim Cramer, Ted Crosbie, Margaret Jennings and Walter McGrath); *Connaught Telegraph* (Tom Courell and P. J. Hennelly); *Drogheda*

Independent (Paul Murphy); Ben Kiely; *Kildare Nationalist* (Eddie Coffey); *Kilkenny People* (John Kerry Keane); *Leinster Leader* (Liam Kenny); Jack Lynch; *Mayo News* (Sean Staunton); *Meath Chronicle* (Jack Davis); *Munster Express* (Kieran Walsh); Cathal and Patsy O'Shannon; RTE (Wesley Boyd, Tom MacSweeney); *Southern Star* (Liam O'Regan; Sandra Woolridge); *Sunday Business Post* (Barbara Nugent); *Sunday Independent* (Aengus Fanning); *Sunday Press* (Michael Keane); *Sunday World* (Colin McClelland); *The Irish Times* (Conor Brady); *Western People* (Terry Reilly).

In Belfast, Mike McComb, head librarian of Century Newspapers, publishers of the *Newsletter*, gave considerable help, as did Walter Macauley, the *Belfast Telegraph* librarian. I am indebted to Kathleen Bell, librarian at the *Irish News*, for her generous assistance. Colin McClelland (*Sunday World*) and John Trew, now a Northern Ireland-based travel writer, gave much appreciated assistance, as did Andy Barclay (*The Irish Times*).

With the Derry chapter, Pat McArt and Colm McCarroll of the *Derry Journal* gave considerable help. My thanks also to Frank Curran, former *Derry Journal* editor. Ivan Montgomery, Derry, helped with material from the old *Derry Standard*. Finally, I must thank Scribes for their work in transcribing the tape cassettes of the radio series.

Introduction

NEWSPAPERS FORM AN EXTRAORDINARY pattern of social, economic and cultural documentation in Ireland, where every national and every provincial newspaper is read with an avidity rarely matched elsewhere in the world. They have been published in Ireland since the mid seventeenth century and many of the national and weekly newspapers published currently throughout Ireland can trace their foundations back to the eighteenth and nineteenth centuries. The industry is still producing new titles that manage to survive hard economic times.

The history of newspapers in Ireland is itself a fascinating study, since no other medium encapsulates the history of the country in such fine detail. But the people who make newspapers, primarily journalists and editors, but not forgetting all the people working in production and printing and distribution, all make up a rich mosaic of individual personalities. Newspapers have generated a sub-culture of their own, yet only rarely are the doings of newspapers and the people who work on them chronicled in as much detail as they themselves record the passing events of the outside world. Newspapers are places of high drama, tension and pace, often enlivened by great good camaraderie, and are the source of many a fine anecdote, improved by constant telling.

Paper Tigers owed its genesis to the RTE radio series of the same name, broadcast weekly between September and December 1992. The individual programmes told a little of the history and some of the anecdotes characterising great newspapers and outstanding moments in their history, as told by some of the participants, mostly journalists and editors, but including certain other people who play such a vital role in the whole business, including chairmen, managing directors and printers. The radio series covered national newspapers published in Dublin and Cork and leading weekly titles in the Republic.

Northern Ireland newspapers were not included in the radio series, so the book has been expanded with two new chapters, one on the Belfast newspapers of the early 1970s, in retrospect rather an interesting and certainly for journalists a very sociable era, despite the ominous overlay of what are called euphemistically the Troubles. The other Northern chapter covers the history of the Derry newspapers. Given the size of that city's population, Derry's contribution to Irish newspaper history has been quite astonishing.

Hugh Oram
Dublin, 29 May 1993

Chapter 1

Characters of the Dublin Newspaper Trade

...

IN THE 1950S AND 1960S, the Dublin newspapers were very prim and highly censored, but marvellous characters worked on them and had great fun. One personality, Mary Kenny, who came into the newspaper business towards the end of this era, is recalled by Cathal O'Shannon, a journalist with *The Irish Times* through the 1950s and into the 1960s.

"She was absolutely outrageous, completely and utterly outrageous", he remembers. In the Dublin newspaper business of the late 1960s, she was a new experience, a breath of very fresh air, and a great innovator, a tough cookie, with the determination to push through change and implement new ideas. The *Irish Press* had never before had this style of features editor, and not only did she bring radically new ideas to the paper, but in doing so she also liked to shock her more staid colleagues by wearing very short miniskirts and perching on the edge of the desk in the newsroom. Other colleagues of the time remember her as being quite a distracting and enlivening influence, and not just for her new thinking. Cathal O'Shannon recollects Mary Kenny, twenty-five years ago, as being similar to a convent girl in full rebellion. Now she is a columnist for such papers as the *Irish Independent* and the *Sunday Telegraph*. "She is completely turned round, almost like a reverend mother herself."

The 1950s and the 1960s were wonderful for the sheer quantity of characters working in the three main Dublin newspaper offices, but in complete contrast to today, what actually went into the papers then was very prim and proper. The characters may have been wayward, especially with drink, but they were given little freedom when it came to what they

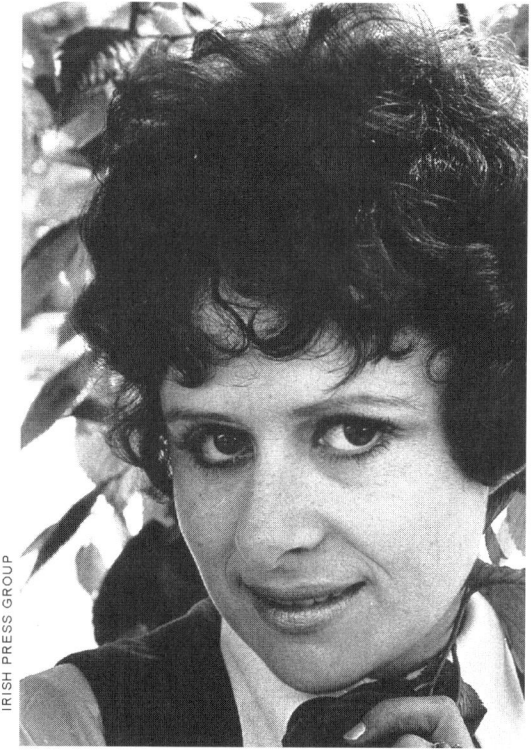

Mary Kenny

Characters of the Dublin Newspaper Trade

Mary Kenny *(centre)* with Maeve Binchy *(left)* at a meeting with seminarians in St Patrick's College, Maynooth, in 1970.

Mary Kenny: in her younger days, a pipe was a frequent appendage.

could write.

"The *Independent*", recalls Cathal O'Shannon, "it seemed to me, and I only came into the business in 1947, had the aura of piety. It was the spokesheet for the bishops of Ireland. The Murphys who owned the newspaper saw to that and the editors of the newspaper, the Gearys and the Rooneys, saw to that too. It was the only newspaper which regularly sent people off to cover pilgrimages to Lourdes and such events. And it was the only newspaper which gave the Easter messages from the various bishops in full. The reporters in the *Irish Independent* always referred to their boss as Mr Linnane and they were referred to in turn as Mr Rooney or Mr Kelly. In *The Irish Times* and the *Irish Press* you got a much greater camaraderie altogether."

Ben Kiely, the novelist and broadcaster, began his newspaper career by working as a leader writer on the *Indo*, easy money for not doing much work. His first novel written when he was still working on that paper was promptly banned. "It was a sort of half disgrace if you weren't banned, because O'Faolain and O'Connor and other people I knew had suffered, so it was a sort of honour to be banned. The actual basic fact was that you lost money." He crossed the river to work in the *Irish Press* at Burgh Quay, but for reasons that had nothing to do with the book banning. Ben Kiely remembers the first time he met one of the greatest of all great characters on the *Irish Press* - Maurice Liston.

"I had written a book called *For a Miracle*; I had stolen the title from Patrick Pearse and I hope he will forgive me. My first night working in the *Irish Press*, I was going up the stairs. I had heard stories about Maurice Liston and he strolled down the stairs and met me for the first time at the bottom of the stairs. He looked at me and he said, 'You hoor, you, you put me in a book.' There was a character in this novel and I had used characteristics that I had heard of about Maurice who was a very big man. I didn't think he was going to murder me, but I was a little bit embarrassed and he lifted me up and put me down again. 'Come out', he said, 'and I will buy you the largest whiskey that a Liston from Newcastlewest has ever bought for a Kiely from Bruff', which was where my grandfather came from."

One famous occasion in the Burgh Quay newsroom produced a Maurice Liston story that has been told and retold many times in the newspaper business by succeeding generations of journalists. "There was a bit of a fire in a convent and Maurice rang up to see what was going on and the Reverend Mother said there was nothing to worry about or some remark like that. Then somebody came up annoying Maurice, and he came out with: 'She said it wasn't worth a fuck', waving this nonsense away from him. It was a perfectly reasonable remark."

The *Indo* was a strict place adhering very closely to the Catholic ethos laid down by the bishops. The *Irish Press* and *The Irish Times* were more free in producing a greater share of characters. Cathal O'Shannon recalls the latter paper. "George McAnnoy was a sports sub in *The Irish Times*, a Belfastman with a very broad, rough, tough Belfast accent and he had the foulest tongue of anyone that I have ever heard in my life. I can use bad language, but I paled into insignificance beside a master like McAnnoy. And he had one of these loud Belfast voices as well; it just wasn't that he used 'f' and 'blind' in every single sentence. On one occasion, on a Sunday night, he was in full blast, giving out to a man called Edgar Brennan, a deputy chief sub, and the language was absolutely incredibly foul. George was in full rant, not repeating himself, and Edgar was this, that and the other. Into the newsroom, behind George and unbeknownst to him, comes the Church of Ireland correspondent, leaving his notes there for the following week, and he comes in and he sees this man and hears this appalling language. The poor cleric's jaw dropped open. George spun around and staggered out of the room; the cleric said to Alan Montgomery, the chief reporter, 'In the name of God, who was that terrible man?' Monty says, 'Oh, take no notice, vicar, that was our cultural correspondent.'

"Indeed, *The Irish Times* seemed to be a shelter at times for the weirdest people. Myles, of course, was Myles. I must say this, too, I never found anything pleasant about the little bugger, quite honestly. I could tell you some stories but they would involve foul language so I am not repeating them. I never saw him in *The Irish Times* actually sober. I never saw him anything but querulous, bad tempered and gruff. You also had other people wandering in and out of *The Irish Times*. You had a marvellous man called John Chichester, Chi Chi, who had been a reporter, but I never saw him write anything in my life. He used to wander around Dublin at night looking into dustbins and finding interesting things in them and bringing them to the men on night-town as gifts. Then you had another little funny old divil called Twitchy Doyle who had been a reporter on

The Irish Times before the First World War. He was a sort of a half pensioner who used to come in and pick up dockets, but he had one unendearing habit, he carried a walking stick and if any woman was in his way as he walked through that lovely old front office in Westmoreland Street, he just hit them and and knocked them out of his way.

"The man who was perhaps the very last in that long line of *Irish Times* characters died not long ago, George D. Hodnett, then our jazz correspondent. 'Hoddy' - I never knew where Hoddy lived - was a bohemian of the bohemians. It must have been in the 1950s that he first came to the notice of *The Irish Times* when he would do little paragraphs for the 'Quidnunc' column; I think Seamus Kelly encouraged him. And jazz was his great love. He was a great jazz pianist and a great aficianado of jazz; he was involved in what might have seemed bohemian activity. He never seemed to wash; he never seemed to have a cigarette out of his mouth. He never seemed to have a halfpenny, yet he always knew where to get a drink. I knew either a cousin or a brother of his who was known as Tappytoes and he was exactly the same. He was a fellow who used to go around on a bicycle with no tyres on it, so you can imagine the noise it made, and a very light little lawnmower. He cut people's lawns for half a crown and maybe a drink or a packet of cigarettes. So they were an odd family, but they were a very distinguished old Dublin family and indeed his grandfather had been a freeman of Dublin. I think they were jewellers in the old days, but where they got 'Hoddy' and 'Tappytoes' I will never know."

Cathal O'Shannon talks about one tremendous personality from the *Independent* group, Raymond Smith, nicknamed "Congo" because of his reporting work there over thirty years ago. "He was a wonderful character, a man of huge exuberance. There have been a number of people I have known in the newspaper business who almost played the front page; they were newspapermen to their backbone and to their front teeth, they thought of nothing else and they had no other existence outside newspapers. One, of course, was the late John Healy. Another one had to be Raymond 'Congo' Smith and another one has been a member of Dáil Éireann for many years, Ted Nealon. They were people who lived, ate and drank newspapers."

There were fabulous people, too, on the fringes of the newspaper business, like the late Pope O'Mahony who got on well with the corpulent

Characters of the Dublin Newspaper Trade

Ben Kiely: when he crossed the river from Independent Newspapers to the *Irish Press* at Burgh Quay, he was greeted by Maurice Liston, a renowned veteran of journalism. Liston welcomed Kiely, whom he had never previously met, with: "You hoor, you put me in a book."

BRENDAN CROWE

Cathal O'Shannon worked for years at *The Irish Times* before going to RTE: he remembers many outrageous antics of old-style journalism.

and amusing Father Senan of the Capuchin Order in Capel Street. Ben Kiely remembers the time that Annie, the caretaker in their premises, got an urgent message from the Pope O'Mahony. When he was passing through Dublin he used an old settle bed they had in their place. One night he was down in Cork and was planning to pass through Dublin, but he had nowhere to sleep, so he sent a telegram to Annie, c/o The Capuchin Fathers, 2 Capel Street, Dublin. "Arriving tonight." He had the key for the ground-floor door, but not the key for the room he was sleeping in. "Arriving tonight, leave bedroom door open, Pope."

To many people's surprise, recalls Cathal O'Shannon, Bertie Smyllie, then editor of *The Irish Times*, was very friendly with the then Archbishop of Dublin, John Charles McQuaid, who nevertheless ruled his diocese with an iron fist in a chainmail glove. But he had his kindlier side. "*The Irish Times*, strangely enough, and R. M. Smyllie in particular, had a very close relationship with John Charles McQuaid. They occasionally dined together, though that may surprise some people. They reasonably often spoke to each other and certainly John Charles McQuaid did a number of favours for R. M. Smyllie and people in *The Irish Times*. I am talking about getting old Twitchy Doyle, for instance, into a home for old people. John Charles personally saw to that, having called up Smyllie, and said he was going to do it. The Church played a huge part, I needn't tell you, in the newspapers in those days; we had to watch ourselves."

In Cathal O'Shannon's time at *The Irish Times*, women reporters were not allowed to cover certain court cases. "You know, even into the 1950s and the 1960s, I could remember coal fires at *The Irish Times*. Certainly in my early days in *The Irish Times* there were only two women reporters, one a girl called June Levine and the other Barbara Dixon, both distinguished subsequently as journalists. June Levine was occasionally sent to cover the courts but she was never sent to cover what were known as dirty cases - rapes, buggery or sex cases of any sort - firstly because it wasn't thought that it would be fit for her virginal ears and secondly because the judges and the barristers didn't like it. Smyllie left a standing instruction that when we were covering these so-called 'dirty cases', although they might not be reported in the newspaper, we were to write them up column by column as if they were going to appear, because he wanted to read them and wanted to know what was going on."

Yet despite the very strict censorship there was great good fun in the

Dublin newspapers in that far-off era, as Ben Kiely reminds us. "I think those days were extremely happy. I wasn't much worried about the censorship, but it did annoy you and the whole lot was a bit of a pain in the backside, you know." Cathal O'Shannon looks back fondly: "I wonder is it my age, I wonder is it people like myself and Ben Kiely looking back on those days? Were they as fun-filled then as I think they were now? I believe they were."

Chapter 2

Vincent Gill and the Longford News

• • •

VINCENT GILL WAS FOUNDER and for nearly thirty years owner and editor of the *Longford News*. He died on 30 April 1976, aged seventy-six, after an extraordinarily bizarre career. Ireland has produced many journalistic characters and eccentrics, but Vincent Gill outperformed nearly all his contemporaries. Just over twenty years ago, Albert Reynolds, now Taoiseach, bought the paper from him.

"I remember asking him how he got into journalism, because he said he had been a member of the Garda Siochana. He was sent to Limerick, himself and a colleague of his, to escort a prisoner to Limerick Jail and they got off the train at Limerick Junction. They went into the bar, had a few jars and they forgot about the prisoner; they lost their man, so Vincent said he got carpeted over it. They were going to dismiss him, so he said he left before he was fired.

"There was the other question of the paper being banned back in the 1940s when he wrote something derogatory about the local bishop or clergy or something and they spoke about him off the pulpit. Eventually, the paper was banned by a court for some reason or another and then he took up writing for the *New Yorker* magazine and eventually brought the paper back on again. I believe the banned version is in the State Solicitor's office in Longford. I haven't seen it but I believe it is there somewhere."

For nearly thirty years Vincent Gill ran the paper singlehandedly, often making up news stories when he was short of copy, devising the most outrageous means of getting advertising and subscriptions and generally creating mayhem in and around Longford. Albert Reynolds continues: "Vincent didn't run it as a business; he would write all the columns himself. He would go around and collect all the advertisements he could. In fact, just for example, on the centre of the floor in the kitchen was a big basin where if you came in with a planning notice or a small notice for the paper, you just threw into the basin whatever you thought the advertisement was worth and if you didn't pay, you still got the advertisement. I know afterwards when I was in the ballroom and hotel business, he used to come around once in a while when, as he said himself, he wanted money to pay the bank manager, to pay some bills. I mean he wasn't a man who ran the newspaper as a business."

But Vincent Gill was a good journalist in his own right. Derek Cobbe, who became editor when the paper was bought by Albert Reynolds and who went on to become owner himself, adds to the saga. "He had a way of getting advertising and subscriptions that I wished to God we could do these days. For example, in an issue he would tell the couple courting on the canal line last week that if they didn't take out a subscription for the *Longford News* their names would be mentioned next week; possibly seven or eight subscriptions were taken out that week. Likewise, he resorted to a kind of blackmail if he found that he wasn't getting advertising. One example was a particular shop in town which didn't advertise for Christmas. So Vincent wrote in the paper that that particular shop had very kindly decided to give all their customers Christmas boxes contrary to the Chamber of Commerce announcement that no Christmas boxes were being given. And of course the shopkeeper was most embarrassed and had to write to all his customers saying the whole thing was a hoax. But at the end of the day Vincent won - he got the ads. But the shop actually closed down as a result of that.

Albert Reynolds continues with the Vincent Gill saga: "I often asked him about how he used to get on with the Revenue Commissioners and he would say, well, he went to see them and told them that if they wanted to come over and share the business with him they could but he wasn't making any money and that was it." But Vincent Gill wasn't just a man to keep a weekly newspaper going by the strangest business methods. He also wrote all the editorial copy, sometimes letting his vivid imagination run riot. At times when news was slack, or Vincent Gill had spent too much time in one of the local pubs, he had other unorthodox ways of filling the space, as Albert Reynolds remembers.

"There was a time, of course, when Vincent wrote all sorts of things about the local gossip. I mean he had a gossip column that was dangerous to say the least. If you ended up in it, everybody knew what your private life was all about. He wrote about chaps who went to dances going home with somebody's daughter or maybe somebody's wife or whatever. As he said himself, there was no point in suing him, he had nothing to get. But he often ended up at the bottom of the canal in Longford, indeed, for some of the articles he wrote, so he was a legend in his time, there's no doubt about it."

Derek Cobbe gives one example: "There was an itinerant wedding in town which attracted a large attendance. He listed the entire diplomatic corps from the President up to the President down as being at the wedding. But then equally if there was a society wedding in town, he listed every single itinerant from near and far as being present at the wedding. Even at St Mel's College past pupils' reunion dinner, he listed everybody he knew from Longford who had ever stayed in Mountjoy Prison as being at the dinner and had them listed as being out for the occasion. He had it in for everybody - he favoured everyone who represented the anti-establishment, the underdog, he was very much a man of the street.

He bought children's confirmation dresses, holy communion dresses, nobody even knew about it until years after he died. He was a most kind and generous man, but a poison pen, an absolute poison pen. Vincent was certainly a man ahead of his time. Had he been around today, I am sure he would write masses of stuff for John Mulcahy for *Phoenix* magazine, for *Private Eye*, or for any of these kind of magazines, but apart from being an excellent journalist, he was certainly a campaigner for the underdog. Vincent had a policy about libel and he was around in the days when people weren't sensitive about things, but they feared Vincent. He always maintained that there was no point in taking an action against him, because when you don't have money, they can't take it from you. That was his policy and it seemed to work for him."

Albert Reynolds recalls how Vincent Gill often borrowed a whole page of news, say, from the *Leitrim Observer* in Carrick-on-Shannon if he wasn't up to scratch in writing that week. "He had his own ways of filling newspapers because he said that it was all just a healthy pastime for people and whether it was made-up stories that kept people happy, fair enough, that's the way he felt about it. He always believed that the best way to pick up news was around the pubs and that's where you would always find Vincent Gill, with the white van parked outside and three or four dogs in

Vincent Gill *(right)* signs his last issue of the *Longford News* in 1974, watched by incoming editor Derek Cobbe.

From left: Albert Reynolds, Jack Davis and Derek Cobbe pictured outside the *Longford News* when Albert Reynolds and Derek Cobbe sold the paper to the Davis family-owned *Meath Chronicle*. Derek Cobbe stayed as editor, later buying back the paper from Jack Davis.

the back. He had cats as well."

"In the little two-roomed cottage which he had in Harbour Row, he slept with his dogs and cats. The dogs and cats rambled around the printing machine. He had one Linotype machine and even before that, he handset all his own type, but the dogs and cats were far more important. In other words, if something had to be bought, it had to be cat food or dog food and printing ink was left until last on the shopping list. He took the dogs and cats everywhere, in fact, and went in and surveyed most of the pubs; they would jump out of the car first, run into the pubs, run around the counter and sit at the counter. Then Vincent would make his entrance and just like royalty, the dogs and cats left first, took up their positions in his car and Vincent entered the car and they ceremoniously drove off to the next pub", explains Derek Cobbe.

Vincent Gill kept the *Longford News* going for nearly three decades. He may have been late some weeks, but he never missed an issue. After Albert Reynolds bought the paper over twenty years ago, Vincent Gill kept writing but straightaway the Reynolds family had to pitch in. "That's true. When we bought it over, Vincent just wrote the column and you had to try and build up production for the paper. I hadn't the same ways and means of doing things as Vincent Gill had. First of all, I wasn't in the business of writing the columns. I was running other businesses, so Eugene McGee used to work part time with me. In the early days of the paper, after I bought it, I think it was the first Saturday it came out, we had nobody to distribute it, so we had to work all night on the Friday night and my wife Kathleen had to distribute the earlier editions. Before the shops opened on a Saturday morning, she was going around the town and the county at about 5.00 and 6.00 and 7.00 in the morning. It was a family affair even at that stage. But it was with the Reynolds, not with Vincent Gill."

Today Longford continues as that rare town in Ireland with two competing local newspapers, the *Longford News* and the *Longford Leader*. Despite many ups and downs the two titles have survived, as Albert Reynolds explains. "There was always, I suppose, put at its mildest, healthy confrontation between them. I think that probably went back over the years. But Vincent Gill didn't want to see the *Longford Leader* – they were old rivals in the town – get a hold of the *Longford News* and close it down. He wanted to see his whole life's work continue into another generation and for that reason he would write what he felt about the *Longford Leader*, and not too kindly at times."

Once again the *Longford News* has changed hands as Paul Healy, the present editor, details. "The paper was founded, in fact, in 1936 by Vincent Gill and after nearly three decades under his colourful ownership and indeed editorship it was of course purchased by Albert Reynolds, the present Taoiseach, in the early 1970s. Since then it was owned by the *Meath Chronicle* and then by Derek Cobbe. In the present day it is owned by the *Midland Tribune* group. We have a very small editorial staff probably typical of small provincial newspapers, just three staff, but under the present system we are a sister newspaper of the *Roscommon Champion* and, of course, that proves beneficial. The paper is printed in Birr in County Offaly. It goes down there on a Tuesday night and hits the shops on Wednesday morning. The paper has probably changed as the country has changed. In Vincent Gill's time, I think the news had even more local input than these days. With society changing, the local media has also changed and has a greater national outlook. In Vincent Gill's time perhaps it was that little bit more intimate."

Vincent Gill was a truly extraordinary journalist and newspaper owner and now nearly twenty years after his death, he has become something of a cult figure. It's hard to talk about the *Longford News* without going back to that flamboyant character as Albert Reynolds often does.

"He was known for having cats and dogs. He always had five or six cats and three or four dogs in the van with him. He wrote the paper and produced it with the help of one young trainer lad in Longford and he distributed it himself. He collected whatever money he wanted to keep him and the paper going or to pay for the newsprint or for a few local schoolboys to deliver the paper around the town. He had his own unique way of producing a paper and indeed getting the message across. He was extremely generous. He lived – and the paper was produced in the kitchen – in Harbour Row in Longford and he always looked after the young people around, looking after them, outfitting them for confirmation or first communion or whatever. He did a programme once on BBC TV's 'Panorama' and I think it all came out there. He told his own story that if he was short of copy he would go to the nearest pub and he would chat up the locals and if he was short of genuine news that week he would make it up himself. There was one great incident that came across in that programme when the researchers for the BBC were over and they picked up a copy of the *Longford News* and the front page said: 'Big fisticuffs, big row at a wedding with the best man ending up in jail, around Ballynacarrigy, just on the borders of Longford and Westmeath.' They spent days and days going around trying to find the people to interview them, but found that no such people existed. So, I mean, Vincent always believed if there wasn't any news around, well make it up.

"There was, for instance, the famous incident when one week he had a big government advertisement taking a full page; the following week he was on the beer, so to speak, in the local pubs doing his rounds and he hadn't time to write enough columns, so all he did was reverse the block and it came out as a blank page in black. The caption up on top was 'Blackout in Drumlish'. You know, he was creative and inventive in that respect. After that BBC programme, a Canadian journalist came over to track down Vincent Gill and to write about him because he was regarded as one of the few remaining old scribes with a style of his own. I had bought the *Longford News* at the time and the people in Canada sent me a copy of the full-page article this guy wrote and I always remember the last line - 'Well, that's Vincent Gill', he says, 'but I failed to catch up with him. I was always one pub behind.'"

We leave Vincent Gill as every journalist would like to be remembered, with some of his best copy brought to life by Derek Cobbe. "'The bride wore knuckledusters and her husband was the best man.' I mean, that was a description of a row at a wedding in the town and Vincent went on in his last little paragraph and said that the 'guards were practically powerless and the citizens came to their aid. They carried one man bodily by arms and legs up the half mile of Main Street to the police station, followed by hundreds of delighted people who had nothing to do, and scores of yelling schoolchildren. This parade was watched by many from shops and private houses and by many barristers and solicitors and witnesses who had just left the Circuit Court. Not since the famous fleadh or the day the Boyle Militia came has the town known such activity.' Then he nicely finished it off by saying that the incident, the second of its kind within a fortnight, may have its court sequel."

Chapter 3

The Sunday World

• • •

THE *SUNDAY WORLD*, LAUNCHED in March 1973, is the biggest selling popular tabloid newspaper in Ireland and is often controversial, particularly for its photographs of underdressed models.

"When a lady from Galway phoned in, she spoke of the scantily clad women who appear regularly on that filthy pornographic newspaper, the *Sunday World*. The appalling answer Father D'Arcy gave was that they were decorative."

"Why are they all jumping on the priest just because the thing was printed in the paper? People buy these papers. They don't have to tell Father D'Arcy to remove those naked women from the *Sunday World*; they are just disgusting." These two opposing points of view were put by listeners to Marian Finucane's "Liveline" programme on RTE Radio 1 in 1986. Reader reaction to the contents of the paper has always been strong. However, Brian D'Arcy has always been one of the most popular columnists in the *Sunday World*, along with Gay Byrne. Gerry McGuinness, who founded the paper with Hugh McLaughlin in 1973 and went on to become executive chairman, explains how the paper came about.

"It came out of a discussion that had started many years previously when Nicholas Leonard, then the founding editor of *Business & Finance* magazine, and myself had looked at the idea of a popular Sunday coloured newspaper. That would have been about 1966, not long after the failure of the *Sunday Review*, simply because it was the wrong product in the wrong market place. But the notion of a popular Sunday tabloid was certainly correct at the time. We looked into the notion at that stage. The numbers appeared right, but the marketing timing was wrong. We took that information, then updated it more or less every year or so after that, and Hugh McLaughlin and myself in mid 1972 felt that the market conditions had improved significantly and sufficiently to allow us to try a launch again. The rest of that year was devoted to planning the launch which took place finally in March 1973. We had a breakeven figure of 200,000 for the first issue which we just exceeded. We never fell below that, so in fact from day one, the product was successful from a consumer viewpoint. It was a much more difficult job to persuade the advertisers that it wasn't just another flash in the pan, a jumped-up copy of some UK import that may have been in the market at the time. So I suppose before it became commercially viable, it would have taken about fifteen to eighteen months, which is not bad, bearing in mind that some newspapers take four, five or six years to become established.

"I suppose the most humorous story I could recall about the launch period was when we were about four or five or six months old. We had established the product right across the country very well, with the exception of Cork which was obviously a major marketing area. So we got together a collection of *Sunday World* issues and sent them in a large brown envelope to Bishop Lucey down there and told him that this newspaper should be banned, as it was bordering on pornography and we signed it 'concerned parents'. The Bishop, God bless him, had the *Sunday World* denounced from all the pulpits in Cork the following Sunday; sales took off and never looked back."

One of the founding journalists on the Sunday paper was Micheline McCormack who joined from the *Sunday Press* very soon after the *Sunday World* was launched in 1973. For her the freedom and fun of the newspaper was something of a revelation. She is now assistant editor on the paper and writes a column which often provokes angry letters from readers. She explains why she made the move to the *Sunday World*.

"In a way the decision was made for me by Gerry McGuinness and Kevin Marron, who had himself worked for the *Sunday Press*, because Kevin just phoned me and said we need you. I came along and then Gerry McGuinness made me an offer I couldn't refuse moneywise and the whole idea of becoming woman's editor became so attractive. I mean, they said, look here, you have this space – just fill it, and I could do what I liked. For me, anyway, that was the most attractive aspect of coming here in May 1973 and still is. Apart from the lawyers checking our copy for libel, I have

Micheline McCormack, assistant editor and woman's editor of the *Sunday World* and an outspoken columnist. She joined the paper soon after it started in 1973; she is pictured here with Michael O'Leary, a former Labour Party leader.

Kevin Marron (*centre*), a former editor and TV columnist of the *Sunday World*, killed in the 1984 Beaujolais Nouveau wine-race plane crash, at Eastbourne in southern England.

this great sense of freedom of being able to write what I like and it is great that twenty years down the line, I still get a kick out of people reacting to what I write. Every single week there are letters calling me all sorts of things - recently, for example, a woman wanted me to be put in jail. A few days later, someone wrote in and said I was sick over a particular issue. Recently I got a letter from the Aran Islands - to think that somebody would go to the trouble in the Aran Islands on their holidays to actually post me a card - saying: 'What is the difference between a piece of furniture in Atlantic Homecare and Micheline McCormack - none - they've both got the same Irish thickness.' So it is great to think that you can still get people reacting in a positive way."

Colin McClelland came from the newspaper business in Belfast to work on the production side fifteen years ago and ended up as editor. He compares the paper then and now. "We have changed it a lot, but if you look at it carefully you see the basic formula is very much the same. I believe that if something continues to work and isn't broken, you shouldn't try to fix it. We had to move obviously with the changing pace of the readership. Some readers grow older and then new readers come in; it is a younger paper and you can't allow it to get old, so you very much keep your finger on the pulse of what younger people consider to be attractive in a Sunday newspaper. I believe they are looking for the same thing that their parents looked for when they started to buy it first: entertainment in the broadest possible meaning of the word. I never believed that the *Sunday World* is a Sunday paper whose duty is to report the news as it happens, because the electronic media cover that very well.

"We certainly have been going out to the people of Ireland and finding out what it is they particularly want to read on Sunday and what sorts of things amuse them, what sorts of things don't amuse them. There was a period we went through when we felt that the *Sunday World*'s long-term tradition of having pretty girls in swimsuits and bikinis may have not been politically correct in the 1990s and might even offend quite a lot of women readers. In fact, all the readership surveys show that the pictures of the girls were the least offensive thing that women readers found in the newspaper; that was a bit of a revelation to us. There has been a major reaction to a columnist, Fiona Looney, who started with us in the autumn of 1992. We have had a phenomenal amount of letters about her column, which has enraged a lot of people and amused an equal amount, always a very good indicator that the columnist is hitting the spot. Fiona is one of those people I have been watching for a while. One of the things I pride myself on is talent spotting and I watched Fiona's work in other newspapers where she worked as a freelance and I thought, 'Here is a talent that fits most easily within the *Sunday World* format rather than anywhere else.' I think some people think that if you read someone and they are controversial and they are funny, that's all they have to be. You have to be a good writer as well."

And Colin McClelland's taste for controversial columnists even extends to religious topics. "Father Brian actually joined the paper before I came on board and I never thought it strange because I read the *Sunday World* long before I joined it, and I saw his column in it. I realised from a newspaperman's point of view that it was a very clever page to have because it took away from *Sunday World* any accusation that it wasn't serious, that it didn't have a social conscience, that it wasn't taking responsibility and it was doing it in a clever tabloid way and that it had a priest writing for it who was actually an incredibly good journalist."

The *Sunday World* has also become the only Dublin-produced newspaper with a big circulation in Northern Ireland, as Gerry McGuinness explains. "Tony O'Reilly and I had a series of meetings at which we decided that it would be interesting to market the *Sunday World* in Northern Ireland to see how successful it would become. It was very successful. We started with a curiosity sale of the Southern edition of about 20,000 and we now sell about 70,000 copies a week in the North."

The *Sunday World* has not been without its tragedies. Kevin Marron, for years editor and quirky TV columnist, wrote his first column for the paper in June 1973. That same year, Jimmy Magee, the RTE sports commentator, wrote his first column for the paper. Marron was killed in the plane crash at Eastbourne in southern England in November 1984 during the Beaujolais Nouveau wine race. An RTE news report the following day described the scene.

"The wreckage is spread fanshaped over some two miles but there is no obvious scoring of the open undulating fields. Pieces of the aircraft almost seem to have dropped vertically in places." Among the other eight people killed was John Feeney, a controversial columnist on the *Evening Herald*. Colin McClelland remembers how he heard the news. "I was lying in bed watching television and I can't remember why I was lying in bed because it was fairly early in the evening. One of our reporters, Dave Mullins, phoned me. I wasn't watching the news and he said, 'Have you heard there has been an air crash in Eastbourne and it's an Irish plane and it was on the Beaujolais Nouveau race.' I was very aware of this trip because I was one of the people who had been invited to actually go on that plane. I think it was just pressure of business that particular weekend that I couldn't get away and the reaction, I mean, I still can't articulate what the reaction was, because I had a very close relationship with Kevin Marron for a good number of years and had a great deal of respect for the man. I suppose I was numb for about a month afterwards. It was very difficult to take in that he and the other journalists on the plane, some of whom I had been with in Paris the previous year, had all just suddenly disappeared in an instant. I still find it very hard to articulate what my feelings were then and even what they are now. They have left a huge gap."

Where does the *Sunday World* go from here, now that there are no more taboos left? Gerry McGuinness answers. "Well, that's a timely question because in the autumn of 1992 the *Sunday World* was relaunched. The aim was to reposition the paper back to where it was in the earlier days. Our research has shown us that we have become too dependent on the sensational investigative story from the mid 1980s. While these stories certainly captured a wide audience for us because of their content, they also ran us into fairly major and serious trouble with litigation. We had a lot of libel actions. The resultant costs ensuing from these, the amount of time they took and the amount of focus that was removed from the day-to-day running of the newspaper convinced us that we really should move away from that ultra-sensational investigative sort of story that was winning us readers but costing us lots of money. So we deliberately softened and moved the product over the last eighteen months or slightly to a side position. We relaunched it on a slightly softer basis in terms of content but with a very strong emphasis now on the sort of basic formula we had when we launched the paper twenty years ago."

But we leave the last word to God and Marian Finucane's "Liveline", where Father Brian D'Arcy addressed his critics. "There is no other paper that will give religion the slot that the *Sunday World* does. Many of the other papers have it stuck in a column here and there, but I have a page each week and it is one of the best-read columns in the paper, I am glad to say, not because of me writing it. I want to get across to people a new image of God. Not a sort of Catholic image of God - just an image of God that might be loving and kind and accessible."

Chapter 4

The Kilkenny People and the Kildare Nationalist

• • •

IN LATE 1992 A venerable weekly, the *Kilkenny People*, celebrated its centenary, whilst simultaneously a rare event in the present-day Irish newspaper industry took place at Newbridge, County Kildare. The *Kildare Nationalist* was born, an offshoot of the *Nationalist and Leinster Times* in Carlow. John Kerry Keane, present managing director and editor of the *Kilkenny People*, explains its genesis.

"There was a vacuum in Kilkenny at the time in 1892; the city was without a newspaper which readily espoused the cause of nationalism. There was a Land League, of course; it was a great movement at the time, but there was no paper that represented the views of those involved in the Land League. Similarly, the Parnellite cause - Parnell was dead just one year. People felt that nationalism should move forward towards striving for freedom and the newspaper was started to echo that feeling and to encourage people to seek freedom; that's what happened."

The *Kilkenny People* was regarded by Lennox Robinson, the Abbey playwright, as one of Ireland's classic weekly newspapers. John Kerry Keane described the celebrations and a little of the paper's history. "Well, it's going for one hundred years obviously and we thought the best thing was to organise a Mass of thanksgiving. The Cathedral Choir at St Mary's had been practising for some months now and they performed the most beautiful Schubert Mass for us. It was tremendous and the Bishop concelebrated and there were representatives there from all the voluntary organisations in Kilkenny, all sporting organisations and friends and colleagues from other newspapers and printing houses right across the country."

Going back a hundred years, what was the competition like when the *Kilkenny People* started?

"Well, there were two other newspapers at the time. One was the *Kilkenny Moderator*, which would have been a unionist newspaper, the other the *Kilkenny Journal*, a paper with a very fine tradition but which was more conservative than the *Kilkenny People* turned out to be. The founding editor was my grand-uncle E. T. Keane who was a controversialist, a man who wasn't afraid to speak his mind in any way and was also very witty. And the public responded to that very well. One of the other founders was P. J. O'Keeffe, who was the mayor of Kilkenny at the time, very much involved with hurling and Gaelic games."

The *Kilkenny People* produced a very special centenary issue which promises to become a collector's item in years to come.

"It comprises a compendium of reports of interesting items over the hundred years. We have articles about how tobacco was thought of; in some of the advertisements in the early days, tobacco was a medical cure so people could feel better. It is quite an interesting publication, photographs of E. T. Keane, soccer teams, the history of Kilkenny, everything that went to make up what Kilkenny is today. The traditional Kilkenny is shown in this one hundred-year centenary supplement," adds John Kerry Keane.

How turbulent has the paper's one hundred-year history been? Has it all been plain sailing?

"I don't think any paper is plain sailing. It is always a very difficult job to produce newspapers on time to a quality you yourself might wish and with the content that the public wants. It is never plain sailing in any newspaper; certainly there have been difficult times. I took over thirty years ago, so I have been at this quite a few years now."

Like all regional newspapers the *Kilkenny People* has been a good training ground for many journalists. John Kerry Keane enumerates some of those famous names. "Frank Geary was the chief reporter here for a number of years and went on to be the editor of the *Irish Independent* for some twenty-five years. Tom Dunne - Tomas Ó Duinn - in *The Irish Times*, is noted for his historical and Irish-language features; Pat Sweeney was industrial correspondent for RTE for many years. Michael Brophy is making a great go of *The Star*."

One of the paper's newest editorial recruits, Carmel Hayes, explains how she came to work in Kilkenny and details some of her duties. "I started with the *Kilkenny People* in May 1991. I did a post-graduate journalism course in Galway and actually did my placement with the *Kilkenny People* and they asked me to stay on. Stories I would have to cover would be Health Board and Corporation stories, general news after that."

The *Kilkenny People* has covered many social issues in an area noted for its progressiveness in such matters. Sean Hurley, news editor, who has been with the paper for thirty years, details the background of one recent case. "We didn't cover the Kilkenny rape case directly, because it was held in the Central Criminal Court in Dublin. But we gave the flak and the fall-out from that case and Lavinia Kerwick herself considerable coverage. She is a tremendous person and now we find that her campaign, her very, very, brave campaign by a little, frail girl whom we interviewed many, many times, has been responsible for changing the law on violence to women. I am very, very happy for the part we didn't necessarily play in it, but for having reported it. She is a lovely person who made a great case for changes in the legislation to deal with violence against women."

In recent times the *Kilkenny People*, which is read by over 100,000 people a week in many parts of the south-east, has taken over two adjoining papers, the *Nationalist* in Clonmel and the *Tipperary Star*. "Our policy would be that we are in competition with them and while they are part of the group, we are still in opposition to one another. We would still try to encroach on their territory and we know that they are trying to encroach on ours. We are in competition with the Clonmel *Nationalist* and the *Tipperary Star* and they with us and that's the way we like it. It keeps us on our toes", says Sean Hurley.

Competition has also come to County Kildare with the long-established *Leinster Leader*, founded in 1880, facing a big challenge from a brand-new paper, the *Kildare Nationalist*, launched in October 1992 by the Taoiseach, Albert Reynolds. The new paper has long roots in the county. Two brothers from County Kildare, John and Patrick Conlon, set up the *Nationalist and Leinster Times* in Carlow in 1883. Its Kildare edition has blossomed into the new paper, one of the very few launches in the industry in recent years. Eddie Coffey, editor of the *Kildare Nationalist*, talks about the parent paper and its long-time editor until nearly a decade ago, Liam D. Bergin, who first joined the paper in the 1920s.

In 1919 the British army suppressed the *Kilkenny People* by removing vital printing equipment.

Taoiseach Albert Reynolds with the first issue of the *Kildare Nationalist* at the official launch in Newbridge on 8 October 1992.

Olivia O'Leary, the RTE and ITV presenter, and a former journalist with the *Nationalist and Leinster Times*, Carlow, with Liam D. Bergin, former editor and managing director of the Carlow paper.

Kildare Nationalist columnist Nell McCafferty, editor Eddie Coffey and executive director and former editor of the *Nationalist and Leinster Times*, Des Fisher, at the launch of the *Kildare Nationalist* in October 1992.

"The *Nationalist and Leinster Times* started over a century ago. Ironically, it was started by two Kildare brothers from just outside Newbridge, the two Conlon brothers. While it was started by two Kildare men, it seemed to centre on Carlow after a short time because it found its level in Carlow and became hugely successful as the main paper there. So from that base in Carlow, it grew out in two directions, mainly County Laois and County Kildare, with a Laois edition and a Kildare edition. It was probably the strongest paper in Laois at that stage in its history and likewise it was very strong in Kildare always, but only in the hinterland of Kildare close to the Carlow border, Athy, Castledermot, that region, and Rathvilly. So really, I mean, while it had a Carlow base it had editions in both of those counties which were very successful", explains Eddie Coffey.

"The Carlow paper has had very distinguished editors; Liam D. Bergin was the editor for many, many years, a doyen of newspaper editors in that he was a character in himself. He was a terribly well-travelled man, a fact that became apparent always in his own columns. He liked to write about world affairs, world trips and whatnot. Desmond Fisher was another famous editor of the past; he is still an executive director of the company. We have had some relatively famous people, journalists, apart from our current crop, like Olivia O'Leary for example, and Des Cahill, to mention a couple of people who are in RTE at the moment. Olivia started her career in the *Nationalist and Leinster Times* and Des worked there for a few years."

Eddie Coffey explains the genesis for the new paper, its staffing and hopes for circulation. "With the Kildare edition, we changed about five to seven pages in the paper, making a good editionalised product for the people of Kildare. But having done a certain amount of market research, we found that despite the fact that it was a Kildare paper, it was regarded as the Carlow *Nationalist* and the people of Kildare wanted a product of their own to call their own. With that in mind, that knowledge of the market research in our minds, we decided to go for the *Kildare Nationalist*, a Kildare paper in total.

"We are based in Newbridge. We have our editorial offices there and we have a stationery shop also on Edward Street at Newbridge which has been there for quite a number of years; the stationery shop is a very successful commercial enterprise, part of the newspaper group. But the main thrust of our push from now on will be in the newspaper end of the business in Kildare with the launch of this new paper. We have two staff journalists based in the Newbridge office and a team of local correspondents around the county. We have columnists, then, who contribute on a regular basis, like Monica Carr covering Naas, Jim Norton covering farming matters and the somewhat controversial Nell McCafferty contributing a weekly column also. So while we have two staff journalists at base, we have a big team covering the entire county, as well as a back-up staff of sub-editors in the Carlow office.

"We have an advertising team of about seven covering the three counties; the good thing about the advertising package that we offer is that while people can advertise in the Kildare paper they can get their advertisement in three editions covering Counties Carlow, Laois and Kildare, a huge advantage particularly in terms of property and entertainment. These segments of the advertising market lend themselves to crossing county borders, in that if there is a farm or land for sale in Kildare, the people on the bordering counties of Carlow and Laois may be as interested as the Kildare people, so it is a good advantage to be able to give a service to advertisers that crosses the county boundaries. We had been printing about 5,500 copies of the Kildare edition; the print run for the first issue of the new paper was close to 9,000 copies. Our target, depending obviously on how people feel about our product, is 10,000 copies a week."

And do you reckon you give the local competition in Naas a good run for their money?

"I reckon the *Leinster Leader* is a little bit shakey in its boots and that shows they feel that we will be successful, but I certainly feel that having visited the newsagents on the night the paper's first issue came out. Some newsagents in Naas and Kilcullen told us that they had doubled their *Nationalist* sales. If I were the *Leinster Leader* I wouldn't be too pleased at hearing that. I am delighted, of course."

Two staff journalists on the paper, Jane Mullins and Barbara Sheridan, both have long experience with what had been the Kildare edition of the Carlow paper. Jane Mullins explains first about the approach putting together the new *Kildare Nationalist*. "Both Barbara Sheridan and myself are journalists on the Kildare team. We have had lots of freedom, we have been able to put our ideas into practice and we find that people like that style of journalism. They like the person coming out into the open - they appreciate our columns in both our Athy page and our Newbridge page that give little snippets of our reaction and their reaction on items of local interest." The paper claims to have been the first regional title to introduce a sex-education column.

Barbara Sheridan talks about the paper's new mascot, Inky, which drew 400 letters from young people before the paper was even launched. "The reaction to him has been marvellous. He is a newspaper cartoon character that I devised myself. We were talking about how we could attract young readers and we came up with the idea of a children's page. From there, we felt we needed somebody who could run the page and Inky came out of that, a cheeky little character. I think he will have a lot to say to the children and they certainly are enjoying him at the moment anyway, from the response we have had to date."

County Kildare is also the setting for another innovative newspaper project, this time in Naas, the county town. This conservation project setting the headlines involving the *Leinster Leader*, FÁS and the county library service is building up a complete database of all items in two local newspapers.

The papers concerned are the *Leinster Leader*, established in 1880 at a time when there was a great flurry of new regional weekly newspaper titles, and still going strong, and the *Kildare Observer*, which started in 1879 and closed in 1935. As Liam Kenny, a journalist with the *Leinster Leader*, explains, compiling this database is a huge task, likely to stretch over several years. But when it is completed, it will mean that historians or researchers will be able to tap in key words and call up on screen any references to any given subject, person or event recorded in those two newspapers. Then the appropriate page or pages can be summoned up on microfilm and, if necessary, printed out.

Not just editorial references provide the data for fascinating social history, as Liam Kenny points out. Very often, the advertisements are just as useful. He gives one example, from an issue of the *Leinster Leader* in 1985, when the Great Southern Railway, a predecessor of today's Iarnród Éireann, advertised return fares of eleven pence from Straffan to Naas for the market. "Sixty pounds' weight of goods will be carried free of charge in both directions", stated the advertisement. "So you could imagine people setting off from Naas with their sacks of potatoes and their baskets of hens, bought at Naas market, and bringing them home to Straffan, supplies for the winter." As he highlighted, files of these two newspapers show pages and pages of amusing advertisements and editorial comment.

Chapter 5

The Irish Times in the 1960s

• • •

SINCE *THE IRISH TIMES* was founded in 1859, few decades have been more exciting within the newspaper than the 1960s, when under the editorship of Douglas Gageby, a great editorial expansion took place. For the first time, women writers came to the fore. Cathal O'Shannon, who worked for years on *The Irish Times* and who is now a TV presenter, brings to mind the style of that era.

"The 1960s saw incredible change in *The Irish Times*. It saw Douglas Gageby come in; it saw Wesley Boyd come in, another most distinguished reporter. It saw Maeve Binchy, Mary Maher and people like that who added excitement without any doubt to *The Irish Times*. *The Irish Times* in some ways may have seemed a rather dull paper but we thought we were great, we thought we were the best reporters. We knew we were the best reporters. We knew we worked on the best newspaper. But Foley and Gageby managed to inject into the newspaper an air of excitement."

In the 1960s all Irish newspapers started changing, a reflection of the upheavals in society as a whole, but the new era was most dramatically visible at *The Irish Times*. "One big change", continues Cathal O'Shannon, "arrived right at the start of the decade. There were no bylines, the best you could ever hope for before 1960 was 'by an *Irish Times* reporter'. Your name never appeared, but in 1960 a couple of things happened. The first Irish troops went to the Congo and I went out ahead of them and Jack White, who was the features editor, went to Cuba because things were happening there, and he got a byline and I got a byline. It wasn't just you got bylines, either. You weren't sent anywhere. To be sent abroad as a reporter on *The Irish Times* or any of the other Irish daily newspapers was really quite an unusual occurrence. The only place I can think of anybody sending people abroad on any regular basis was the *Irish Independent*, which always sent a reporter on the Dublin Diocesan visit to Lourdes, year in and year out, but *The Irish Times,* of course, didn't bother with things like that."

Alan Montgomery, who had been news editor for many years, followed Alec Newman as editor. Newman himself had succeeded R. M. Smyllie on the latter's death in 1954. Montgomery was responsible for many forward-looking improvements in the paper, but the real impetus for change came with that formidable duo, Douglas Gageby and Donal Foley. Douglas Gageby had been founding editor of the *Evening Press* and became editor of *The Irish Times* towards the end of 1963. Donal Foley, who had worked in the paper's London office, came home to Ireland to become news editor. The two unleashed a creative volcano rarely seen before in the history of Irish newspapers. Wesley Boyd, then diplomatic correspondent of the paper, later RTE's head of news and now director of broadcasting developments, was a close friend of Donal Foley, a teacher's son from Ring in County Waterford.

"I think it was his enthusiasm for everything; he infected other people in the paper with that enthusiasm. He made them feel that journalism was a worthy thing to be in, that it should be associated with the everyday life of the country, that it should hold the life of the country up to the public and investigate it, examine it, tease it out in his own column 'Man Bites Dog', make fun of it. It became a much more lively newspaper, but it is only fair to say that newspapers generally were evolving in that direction. But Donal perhaps gave a greater kickstart to it in *The Irish Times* than was happening elsewhere at the time."

But before all those stimulating editorial ideas could be put in place, financial foundations had to be laid. Douglas Gageby describes the outward looking attitude of the board of directors and the work of someone who is there to this day, Major T. B. McDowell, chairman and chief executive.

"I am not sure there were very radical changes editorially. The mission was this: whatever about *The Irish Times* being largely a Dublin newspaper in the past, we wanted to go out to all corners of Ireland for everyone to read. One of the shifts was, indeed, that we suddenly looked at the North of Ireland and decided that we weren't covering it properly. There was a parliament in Dublin, there was a parliament in the North of Ireland. It may not have been much of a parliament; in fact, the local papers used to tell us: 'You are wasting your time covering it, it's only a county council.' But there were fifty, sixty or seventy Irish people there arguing about what was going on in the island. We suddenly said, 'Dammit, what have we been doing all our lives? We must read and see what they are doing, and if people don't want to read it, they can turn over the page.'

"So we would often carry a full page of Stormont in those days and a page on the Dáil, and that I suppose was the biggest shift; even the Belfast papers said we were mad. But we went on doing it - Fergus Pyle first, then Henry Kelly, then Eileen O'Brien, a wonderful reporter, and that was in many ways the biggest shift. We took a very close look at politics, of course, and Donal steered us into his Gaelic culture, which I suppose culminated in Merriman. But it was above all an opening up to, as we saw it, all of the activities to all of the people on this island. That is how we saw it and it worked, apparently, and it could have worked earlier, I believe, if the board of *The Irish Times* in the 1950s had had that expansionist view. I believe it could have started earlier, given that they had the writers; they had some very fine writers on *The Irish Times* then, but it was starved of resources until about the early 1960s."

Under the new regime, much of the new blood came into the paper from unorthodox sources. Wesley Boyd remembers Donal Foley's role. "He was particularly good at recruiting women journalists and again he made quite an impact in Irish journalism because he recruited bright young women journalists. Up until then women journalists had been inclined to be associated with what you could broadly term women's events, like fashion shows and bring-and-buy sales. But Donal insisted that they should work on the same level as male journalists, cover the same things - politics, social affairs, whatever was happening."

Mary Maher came to the paper from the United States on what she thought was a temporary basis. "I came on speculation. I was working on the *Chicago Tribune*, where I was very fed up with being ghettoised with women's features. I thought, well, perhaps if I worked somewhere else for a year I would get extra credentials. So I came to Ireland hoping to work for a year because I was interested in Ireland, like all Irish-Americans. And *The Irish Times* took me on for three months at fifteen pounds per week on probation. They never told me whether the probation was over, so I assume that it is. I found that I was far freer in *The Irish Times* doing the kind of story that interested me than I would have been in any American

The Irish Times in the 1960s

Douglas Gageby during a presentation with Conor O'Clery at *The Irish Times*.

Douglas Gageby, a long-time editor of *The Irish Times*, who retired in December 1986. He is seen here being presented with a portrait of himself by Basil Blackshaw by Major T. B. McDowell, chairman and chief executive.

Paper Tigers

R. M. Smyllie, editor of *The Irish Times* until 1954.

Alan Montgomery, editor of *The Irish Times* in the early 1960s.

Alec Newman, editor between R. M. Smyllie and Alan Montgomery, in the 1950s.

Mary Maher, who joined *The Irish Times* from Chicago in the mid 1960s.

Conor Brady, editor of *The Irish Times*.

The late Bruce Williamson, who worked at *The Irish Times* from the end of the Second World War until 1989.

Maeve Binchy was a teacher until she was recruited to *The Irish Times* in the 1960s.

The Irish Times in the 1960s

As news editor, Donal Foley was responsible for recruiting many fine women journalists to the paper in the 1960s.

Wesley Boyd, who was diplomatic correspondent of *The Irish Times* until the early 1960s when he joined the then new RTE television service, becoming head of news. He is now director of broadcasting developments there.

paper. *The Irish Times* was a small, liberal, eccentric newspaper which was bursting with ideas and they didn't put any barriers in my way. So oddly enough I was free to do what I wanted to do; I never could go back because I got too involved in the job and the work and the changes that were happening.

"That was the autumn of 1965, I remember. I was very lucky, I think, to arrive just at the moment when things were about to change. Maeve Binchy came after me. Mary Cummins, Nell McCafferty, Elgy Gillespie; after that it was Ella Shanahan, Geraldine Kennedy, a good many not from the traditional background at all. There wasn't much of a traditional background for women. Mary Cummins wrote such a good letter of application that Donal rang her up and said, 'Come and see me' and Nell wrote a couple of feature pieces to start. Donal was away ahead of his time in hiring women to do work that wasn't associated with the traditional women's page. Nearly every day a great gang of people went out to lunch, eight or ten of us, including Maeve Binchy and myself, and we would end up in the basement of the Harp Bar at O'Connell Bridge having long, argumentative lunches, and I mean shouting sometimes, and people marching in and out, cooling off about things, talking about what to write for the paper. Then you would go back to work and get to it. And after work, this discussion would continue as well, it was a lot of fun and great times, wonderful times. There was always something new, and new, exciting ideas which you would take hold of and run with."

The older generation of journalists rose just as strongly to the challenge, including Seamus Kelly who wrote "An Irishman's Diary" and Bruce Williamson, brilliant poet, critic and journalist who played an often unseen but crucial backroom role.

"Not a bit of bother on either one of them. You have just mentioned two spectacular people. Bruce is a terrible loss. Even now he is missed; when you had Bruce, you didn't need seventeen dictionaries. He was wonderful. There was never a wall of resistance to any new idea. They were two intelligent people. They were part of the whole transformation", remembers Mary Maher. Wesley Boyd recalls Donal Foley's not always organised ways of working. "He was extremely argumentative but again he was open to ideas and if he liked the ideas that were put forward, he would support them all the way."

How does he remember Donal Foley personally?

"Great good humour, great charity, great friendship. I never met anyone who disliked him. He had great loyalties. He was very loyal to the Irish language, for example, and he ensured that we got away from the old tokenism. Anyone who wrote in Irish wrote about contemporary affairs, not about folklore or folk music, but he wanted to have Irish used to project what was happening in the Ireland of the day. Indeed, he was responsible for starting the present 'Tuarascáil' page which still exists until this day."

Life at *The Irish Times* in the 1960s wasn't all work and serious talk, as Mary Maher details. "Again, I remember one day Maeve Binchy was sitting behind the women's desk on the phone to somebody and suddenly she ran out, disappeared, leaving the phone on the desk still cackling. I looked across the room and I saw somebody come in she particularly didn't want to see; she hid behind the door and I was left to walk across the room and say no, no, she is not in right now, while this phone was lying on the desk going squak, squak, squak. There was another famous time when one of our reporters, whom I won't mention because he is still around, too, another great reporter who got so impatient with the ringing telephone that he stood up on the desk and cut the wires. They hung there for years, just the dangling wires, and we always waited for the Department of Posts & Telegraphs to come around. He just put the phone in the drawer. There was, if you like, a very eccentric, irreverent and slightly anarchic air to the newsroom."

The 1960s are thirty years ago. The newspaper business has changed fundamentally and irrevocably. Conor Brady, present editor of *The Irish Times*, brings the story up-to-date. "It used to be said that every time a name appeared in the deaths' column of *The Irish Times*, the circulation of the paper went down by one. That happily isn't the case. We are quite happy with the way the circulation of the paper is going. We don't have circulation targets. We are not aiming for any particular circulation or readership level. If we go up a little bit every year, then we think we are going in the right direction and that's the sort of circulation and readership that stays with you. It is not an ephemeral thing, so we are not actively out to beat people into picking up the paper. If more and more people throughout this society like what we are doing, respond to the sort of paper that we are, respond to the sort of values we try to represent and if they stay with us, then that makes us very happy."

He talks about the almost daily supplements in the paper with the further recent extension of *The Irish Times*'s printing capacity. Larger papers, more colour and more supplements are now possible. "Well, it is one of the developments that has taken place. It is possibly the most vivid development but we have also, for example, very significantly developed our international news network with a new bureau in Moscow, Washington and now Africa. I think we will continue to expand our international network. We will also be producing, I hope, some additional supplements. It is very difficult to give a precise list of how one ranks those things in priority."

Whatever the present and the future of *The Irish Times*, we have been concentrating on the 1960s. So we will leave the last words to two of the people who were central to that decade, Douglas Gageby and Cathal O'Shannon.

O'Shannon: "Great fun. I don't regret a moment of it. In many ways it was a bloody privilege to work on *The Irish Times*. It was the greatest fun, the greatest gas. It was a great life." Gageby: "It was all fun, all fun with a bit of business."

Chapter 6

The Skibbereen Eagle and the Southern Star

• • •

SINCE THE FIRST NEWSPAPER was published in Ireland in 1649, no newspaper has achieved such world-wide notoriety for one remark as the old *Skibbereen Eagle*, for over sixty years incorporated in the *Southern Star*.

"It will still keep its eye on the Emperor of Russia and all such despotic enemies, whether at home or abroad, of human progression and man's natural rights, which undoubtedly include a nation's right to self-government. Truth, liberty, justice and the land for the people are the solid foundations upon which the *Eagle*'s policy is based."

The *Skibbereen Eagle*, or otherwise the *Cork County Eagle* and *Munster Advertiser*, on 5 September 1898 was "keeping an eye on the Czar of Russia". With that grandiose but almost throwaway remark in the leader column of the long defunct *Skibbereen Eagle*, no phrase from an Irish newspaper in over 300 years of publishing has since achieved such worldwide fame. Nearly a century later the expression is still widely used. Over sixty years ago the renowned, not to say notorious, *Skibbereen Eagle* was taken over by its deadly rival - the *Southern Star* - in the West Cork town. Liam O'Regan, present owner and editor of the *Southern Star*, explains how that Czar of Russia phrase got propelled into world renown.

"I imagine it became a bit of a laughing stock in a sense, because it sounded a bit ridiculous for a small weekly paper to be watching the Czar; it was indeed mentioned in the House of Commons by Tim Healy and I imagine that prominence would have broadcast it even wider. Fred Potter, the editor and owner, embellished it with all kinds of stories, most

Paper Tigers

Staff outside the *Southern Star* offices in Skibbereen, Co. Cork, in the early years of this century, probably between 1910 and 1917. The only member of staff who can be positively identified is Mike O'Sullivan (*fourth from right*), who continued with the firm when it moved to its present address in Ilen Street in 1932, and who spent the rest of his working life with the newspaper.

Frederick Peel Eldon Potter, owner and editor of the *Skibbereen Eagle*, usually known simply as "Fred". He wrote the famous leaders about keeping an eye on the Czar of Russia.

of which he made up to do with vicious murders in China and all sorts of nefarious goings on, which were indeed very imaginative. They can be found in the files of the *Eagle* and which we ourselves published some time ago in the centenary issue of the *Southern Star* in 1989."

Confusion still exists about the origins of the phrase and the date on which it was first used, as Liam O'Regan explains. "We have evidence in editorials from several years in the 1890s, but my feeling is that it was much older. There is evidence of an editorial in 1871 but it originally went back even further to Father Prout. So I think it was a phrase adopted by Potter rather than invented by him, and to that extent he capitalised on it and he made it his own."

Frederick Peel Eldon Potter, owner and editor of the *Skibbereen Eagle*, certainly milked the expression for all it was worth, as can be seen in this extract dated 5 November 1898. "The Emperor of all the Russias is again at his fiendish tricks. This time, aiming at England, he has sent his aged and respective grandmama Victoria, by the Grace of God, almost mad with his evil designs on China. The young and enlightened Emperor of that unhappy region, China, has been murdered. They commenced operation by burning his eyes and setting fire to his pigtail. Next, they cut off his monkey nose. Then they removed his pearly teeth, pulled out his tongue, chopped off his ears, denailed his toes and cut his throat. Slow poisoning caused a lingering death which lasted for a month. The Russian has taken a move that will set all the world ablaze with war torches. Yet we are told this is the man of meekness who seeks the disarmament of humanity. What a lying hypocritical wretch! Would he not be better described as the Prince of Darkness, this cloven footed monster!"

Present-day opinion columns by comparison are the very model of sedate calm. Unfortunately for Potter, this most colourful of his many editorials on the Czar of Russia was written on the strength of what turned out to be a false news report. The Potter family who set up the *Skibbereen Eagle* in 1857 were of Welsh origin. Before the *Eagle* they ran a paper in Kinsale called with delightful insouciance the *Kinsale Bee*. In the early 1870s they ran a daily paper in Cork City for a couple of years, the High Tory *Irish Daily Telegraph* which went bankrupt in quick order. Not to be outdone, Frederick Potter returned to the *Skibbereen Eagle* where his father had been minding the shop in his son's absence.

Later, Frederick Potter dabbled in all kinds of enterprises including auctioneering and the hotel business as the name of the present-day Eldon Hotel in Skibbereen reminds us. The boastful and grandiloquent Potter once described the *Skibbereen Eagle* as the largest penny paper in the world.

The *Eagle* was rampantly unionist so the *Southern Star* was set up as a nationalist counterbalance. For many years the paper was controlled by the Catholic clergy in the locality. A local priest, Reverend Monsignor John O'Leary, was its chairman. Then nationally minded shareholders including Michael Collins took it over. Seamus O'Kelly, author and journalist, later editor of the *Leinster Leader* in Naas, was one of its editors. The most famous of its early editors was Ernest Blythe who was a subsequent Minister for Finance and who became hated for cutting a shilling off the old age pension in 1931. In 1921 Joseph O'Regan became a shareholder, eventually buying out the paper in 1949, by which time the *Southern Star* had long since taken over its rival. Liam O'Regan, son of Joseph, explains how long he has been running the paper.

"I suppose you could say since my father died. He was the boss up to 1975 and I had been there for about sixteen years before that, so I am here quite a long time. We have a reasonably good sale in Cork City and a smaller sale in East Cork. But our main area would be from the city west and north as far as Ballyvourney and Blarney; on the western side we go all the way out to Mizen Head and to Castletownbere and we even have a small sale in parts of South Kerry, but really we are the West Cork, Mid Cork and South Cork paper, rather than East Cork."

Over the years, some distinguished media personalities have begun their careers on the *Southern Star*. Tom MacSweeney is Southern correspondent of RTE and also presenter of the "Seascapes" programme on Radio 1. "I joined the *Southern Star* in 1962, moving from the post of trainee reporter on the *Cork Examiner*. The reason for going from a daily to a county weekly was quite simple; first of all, the *Southern Star* offered five pounds a week plus my stamp, whereas I was being paid only three pounds in the *Cork Examiner* and my stamp. Then there was also the opportunity to write more regularly for the paper because in those days on a daily newspaper like the *Cork Examiner* the trainee didn't get to write very much for the paper. Then, of course, there was a certain fascination about working for the county newspaper, as the *Southern Star* was described in the job advertisement. It was a step up, not being a junior reporter any more. After about six or eight months of journalism, the

Typical cuttings from the *Skibbereen Eagle* in the late nineteenth century. It was as renowned for its many changes of title as for its self-advancement and aggrandisement.

move came as a valuable step forward.

"I remember being interviewed by Joe O'Regan, who was then the proprietor and father of the present editor and owner, Liam O'Regan. He interviewed me in the foyer of the old Victoria Hotel in Patrick Street, not a particularly private place. But anyway, I must have passed the interview because I was offered the job. I remember getting a page of copy paper lined in Joe's careful handwriting, giving me the fixtures I would have, such as Monday, Cork County Council, Tuesday, Midleton Urban Council, Wednesday, Macroom Court, and so on. But at least that was taking me around the county. I was also provided with a scooter with only one seat."

Today, staff at the paper include John Hamilton, long-serving business manager. Leo McMahon is a well-regarded reporter who has worked there for about eighteen years; more recent editorial arrivals are Jackie Keogh and Jean Kelly. West Cork is home to an international artistic community, a fact reflected in the *Southern Star*'s arts coverage. Just two of the big names often resident in the area are writer Deirdre Purcell, who has a house on the Beara Peninsula, and film producer David Puttnam, who has a house near Skibbereen. A star writer working freelance for the *Southern Star* is Sandra Woolridge, who lives in Drimoleague. She describes how she started with the paper.

"I walked into the office one day and said, 'You know, I would like to do personality profiles.' They weren't doing any personality profiles at all at the time, and I think the editor, God bless him, was delighted with the idea and said, 'Yes, please go ahead and do them.' And I did my first piece about the water diviner who lived just next door to me. I think the basic reason why there is such a broad spectrum of things covered in the *Southern Star* is that editorially they are open. They are conservative, yes, but also very, very open to the arts and to quality writing. If there is any value in writing, they will see it and use it, and really it doesn't have to slot into anything."

She also reveals why she is Sandra Woolridge for the *Southern Star* and Sandra MacLiammoir for the *Sunday Independent* and other publications, and her connection with Dick Emery, the comedian. "I started writing under the name of Sandra Woolridge in Ireland because I was actually married at the time. I am separated now for six years and I very quickly reverted to the Irish spelling of my maiden name, which is

McWilliams. So of course having been born in Britain, I romanticised everything about Ireland and my presence here, so I decided that I would henceforth be MacLiammoir, little realising the impact that the name would have. I just saw this as my name and of course people often ask me whether I am related to the great Micheál, whom everybody apparently adored, and I have to say that no I am not but that I am closely related to Dick Emery. So it's not one drag queen but the other."

Sometimes, as Tom MacSweeney concludes, there can be too much truth in the news. "Pubs have been a great source of news. What I didn't realise at the time, of course, was that there seemed to be an almost unstated observance in reporting cases of breaches of the licensing laws, that you didn't use the names of the 'found-ons' who were on the premises, the customers who were there after hours. You didn't use their names. In my initial few days with the *Southern Star*, I did use the names. I believe that after one court case in a local village where my report gave not only the name of the publican but the name of every of found-on of twenty who was on the premises, there were great sales for the paper in that particular village in that particular week."

Chapter 7

Hot Metal Technology

...

"ALWAYS WHEN I THINK of paper technology I think of noise. I miss the noise because the noise was very exciting in a newspaper. Even when you went into the composing room there was the rattle of anything up to forty or fifty Linotype machines setting up the metal type, one hell of a din. The noise of metal being put together in the chases was accompanied by people shouting at each other. That's all gone now. People sit around banks of computer terminals, typing softly, softly into the system." Michael O'Toole of the *Evening Press* casts a backward glance at the ancient technology in the newspaper business.

This chapter is about the huge change in the way newspapers are made now that computers have taken over. For a couple of hundred years, the methods used to print newspapers remained the same, just becoming more automated. Hot metal was not a rock band but the molten metal, mostly lead, which bubbled away until it was turned into type for printing. The men on the keyboards made up lines of type, which in turn were used to compose pages, all the while accompanied by various strange rituals. Newspapers were originally printed from wooden letters made up by hand, then from metal. The process became more and more mechanical but the typesetters, known as comps, lived in an enclosed social order amid the dirt, heat and noise. These kings of the old style craftsmen worked amid an incessant din.

Today the computer has taken over every newspaper in the country and the business of typesetting all the copy is silent, just the quiet clickings of the modern keyboards. The old ways have been swept away along with the comps and their arcane way of life. Two of the hot metal typesetting machines can be seen in Dublin, one in the front office of Independent

Newspapers, the other in the *Irish Press* group. These machines stand like beached dinosaurs from a long forgotton industrial age. Hopefully, when the new National Print Museum opens in the old Garrison Chapel at Beggars Bush in Dublin, some of the old newspaper equipment will be there as working, living museum pieces. Sheila Weyman is responsible for the editorial production on many feature pages in *The Irish Times*. She sampled the old way of working before making the move into new computer screen-driven technology.

"Yes, I worked for some years in the *Irish Independent* and that was total hot metal when I went in there. I had freelanced in *The Irish Times* which was computer setting, and not hot metal. So I went to the *Irish Independent*; it was like a step backwards into this older world of hot metal and all the Linotype machines. It was a dirty, noisy environment but I suppose the hard newspaper men would say that it has lost all of its character because the dirt has gone. It's not like a real newspaper anymore, they say, it's so quiet and clean. Nowadays, if a picture is not the right size or slightly long you can just slice it with a blade, but in those days you had to take the block. It was on a heavy metal block, and you had to physically carry it to a big guillotine machine which was operated by your foot. It was mostly men down there and in fact I was the first woman sub working at night. So I had to physically carry the block over and get it into the guillotine machine, tuck up my skirt and work the guillotine machine with my foot to lob off an inch off a picture."

By tradition only men worked the machines that produced the typesetting for newspapers. They went by typed or handwritten copy - sent down from the sub-editor's table. Once a reporter had written a story the unseen backroom staff of the newspaper swung into action.Until recent years, men had always totally dominated every area of newspaper production, sub-editing, typesetting and printing. Sheila Weyman came into the job at the very moment that the change from hot metal to computers was happening.

"I was obviously a bit of a novelty in the caseroom for a while, but they were very kind to me. And now there are quite a lot of women around at night for production."

Victor Styles was a long-time father of the chapel for the comps in *The Irish Times*. He explains how newspaper printing originally developed from the religious life. "Oh, definitely there were no women allowed into

A battery of Linotypes at work producing hot metal setting in Independent Newspapers, Dublin.

Hot metal setting at the *Cork Examiner*, with Walter McGrath (*right*), the man responsible for the *Holly Bough*.

In the stoneroom at Independent Newspapers, Dublin, Brendan O'Farrell (*left*) and Paddy Murray, who is now an outspoken and humorous columnist on *The Star* newspaper, a joint venture between Independent Newspapers and Express Newspapers in Britain, and a rare launch among Irish newspapers.

With the old-style technology, newspaper headlines had to be set in metal manually. Here, Brian Grehan is making a headline in the old-fashioned way for the *Irish Independent*. Like all other Irish newspapers, those in Independent Newspapers now use computerised typesetting.

the printing section at all. As a matter of fact, I can remember when permission had to be sought for a female to come into the room; it was called hallowed ground and that, of course, goes back to the stage where printing actually originated in the monasteries and was run totally by monks, so naturally enough they had no association with the female sex at all. The tradition was actually one of those things passed down from one generation to another. That's where the Father of the Chapel comes from; in every printing office in Dublin, the section is headed by the Father of the Chapel rather than a shop steward. He is actually a shop steward but they call him the Father of the Chapel. To some extent it was like the Masonic Order. There were a lot of restrictions."

He remembers when he first began work on the night shift of newspapers during the emergency period of the Second World War.

"I commenced working in the newspaper business as an apprentice in the year 1942, during the war. At that time, the censorship was very, very strict on account of the war, and everything prior to publication had to go to the Censorship Board to be passed. Consequently, we were late every morning in going to press because we had to wait until the return of the censored material. Even then, portions had to be taken out and other portions added into it. So we set up in advance a lot of short stories to accommodate holes in the page, as the saying was at that time, so that we could put our paper to bed very quickly after we got the okay from the Censorship Board."

The emergency years were not the only times of panic in newspaper production. Alfie Dalton, now retired and living in Glenageary, County Dublin, worked as the caseroom overseer in the old Dublin *Evening Mail* which closed down in 1962, mainly because of competition from the *Evening Press*. He remembers the set-up in the old *Mail* offices at the top of Parliament Street, across from City Hall.

"I think there were about seven or eight Linotypes, pretty old models. Of course, during my time they were all replaced; we had about twelve or fourteen machines eventually and we got a lot of work out of them. Saturday was a very busy day for the sports. There was a real push and we used to do a *Sports Mail* as well on the Saturday; we would get an hour's overtime and we went hell for leather. Down in the caseroom there was just copy, often handwritten, thrown at you; you would have to sort it out and set it. We had a *Sports Mail* out in the streets at 7.00 at night. It was an extremely noisy process; you had maybe thirty machines running at the same time and every one of them were clinkety clank all the time. It was a very noisy process indeed, and a dirty one as well."

Hot metal typesetting machines vanished from use as decisively as steam engines. The people who had to work the old-style printing equipment in the Dublin daily papers and the weeklies in the rest of the country have little sentiment or nostalgia. Romantic notions are left to the outsider. The old days when the comps wore their bowler hats into work are gone, without regret.

"I reckon that it is very much better, yes. I am very much in favour of it, except for the fact that there are not so many people required to operate the system. But certainly it is much cleaner, much neater, much quieter. I would be very much in favour of the new methods", concludes Victor Styles.

"Yes, you really appreciated the new technology when it came. The leap was much greater in the *Irish Independent*, but was more staggered in *The Irish Times*. I don't think I am old enough to be sentimental about it, unlike some of the older people. No, there is nothing I would miss about it", adds Sheila Weyman.

Johnny Hughes, the chief sub-editor of *The Irish Times*, explains how the new systems have changed methods of working in the newspaper business. "I think perhaps one of the most dominant features of the technology itself is that before, from the time I began working in editorial, it had been that way from the time I began, going back into the time when God was a boy. From now on, I think, we are into changing technology and it will be constantly updated for the foreseeable future."

He also explains how newspapers now put together by electronics will work more closely with other electronic media. "I expect that there will be a greater liaison between all of the media throughout the world, with the result that something that is on television at any given time will probably be available to newspapers as well. If, for example, you have President Clinton making a speech, you would be able to 'translate' instantly from the television, getting photographs from the screen. The other development is colour. I think that it is almost inevitable that newspapers will present any graphics and pictorial content in colour. I have noted that it is particularly effective in simple things like weather charts; if you have blues and reds as opposed to just black, white and grey, the presentation is clearer. Most children growing up now, as opposed to my own childhood, are living in a coloured world, with less black and white."

One big advantage of the new technology is that production has been greatly speeded up. In a recent example from *The Irish Times* a late story broke during the 1992 currency crisis. The reporter wrote his piece at 4.50 in the morning and the last edition of the paper for circulation in Dublin was ready for the newsagents and the street vendors by 5.30 am.

"Normally we aim for getting off the stone at 3.00 in the morning, which would mean that we would be printing about 3.30 am, but we have leeway and we can slow down the presses if we know that there is a late story coming, so we get a greater number of city edition copies. We don't compete like we used to with the electronic media because it is far quicker, but we can pick up on the story in greater detail the following day. Now we aim more for continuity in how we cover stories, rather than immediacy. Well, you can't just bash it out of the typewriter and hope that somebody keying it in downstairs will know what you meant. You have to get it exactly right", concludes Johnny Hughes, spelling out the precision of the new newspaper technology.

Chapter 8

Belfast's Papers in the Early 1970s

• • •

NEWSPAPER LIFE IN BELFAST in the early 1970s was exciting, but dangerous, fun mixed with daily terror, and glamourised by the presence of so many journalists, not just from the Manchester and London offices of the UK national papers, but from the Dublin papers and indeed from newspapers further afield, in Europe and the US. The combination proved intoxicating for many reporters covering Belfast at that time, and as it turned out it was almost the last expression of good times among people working on the Belfast papers.

Some excitement centred around the *Sunday News*, which had been established in 1965 by the *Newsletter* and said by cynics, with which the newspaper business is infested, to have been an attempt to woo a largely Catholic readership. The old *Belfast Weekly Telegraph* newspaper, which had been closed down in 1964, was continued as *Cityweek*, and finally, briefly, as *Thursday*, by Mortons of Lurgan until 1971. The *Irish News*, too, had a weekly publication; it and the *Cork Examiner*'s weekly paper closed in 1981. They were the last of the breed in Ireland.

By the early 1970s, the Belfast newspaper trade had recovered from the trauma of the *Northern Whig* closure in 1963, and the displacement of its journalists and other staff. In 1961 the *Belfast Telegraph* had passed into the hands of the Canadian media tycoon Roy, later Lord, Thomson, the man who was immortalised by describing commercial television as a licence to print money.

He said that the attacks in Belfast against his honour and integrity had never been made against him anywhere else, and he vowed never to set foot in the city again. Lord Thomson was as good as his word, although his son Kenneth, himself later Lord Thomson, who took over the

Thomson organisation from him, did visit the Belfast paper from time to time.

The *Belfast Telegraph* acquisition was the first breach in the local ownership of the Belfast papers. As long as anyone could remember, the Hendersons owned the *Newsletter*, and the Cunninghams controlled the *Northern Whig*, while the *Irish News*, produced and published at the other end of Donegall Street from the *Newsletter*, was owned by the McSparrans. Dr Daniel McSparran, chairman, and his sister Mary, company secretary, were killed in a road accident in 1981. After a two-year hiatus, control of the paper passed to James J. Fitzpatrick, the managing director. A development in 1974 epitomised the spirit of optimism of that decade, despite the Troubles. Arthur Boucher and Brian Croley from the *Newsletter* took over Morton Newspapers in Lurgan, although later, the Morton family was to regain its control of an undertaking that had started most modestly and has built up over the last three decades to encompass half of the weekly newspaper titles published in Northern Ireland.

After the shock of the Thomson takeover of the *Belfast Telegraph* came the prolonged industrial relations problems at the *Northern Whig*, founded in 1824. Many distinguished journalists worked on the paper at some stage, including Wesley Boyd, who was later diplomatic correspondent of *The Irish Times* before moving to RTE, where he was head of news for many years and is now director of broadcasting developments. Mervyn Pauley, long-serving political editor of the *Newsletter,* also worked on the *Whig*, and so too did Norman Ballantine, for long associated with the same paper, as did Ralph Bossence, who transferred to the *Newsletter* in 1947.

Bossence, known in the newspaper business as "Bud", had a circuitous upbringing, born in Belfast but educated in Detroit. In 1964 he began his well-regarded humorous column on the *Newsletter*, "As I See It", which continued for nearly ten years, until his demise. A large, shambling, amiable man, who lived a bachelor existence off the Lisburn Road, he had one of the best collections of jazz records in Ireland. His favourite hostelry was the Duke of York, just off Lower Donegall Street, and then the "branch office" of the *Newsletter*. Quite often, journalists from that paper would slip in before opening time for quick refreshments before another day's slog.

One of those early imbibers was Kay Kennedy, who died in early 1993. Her estranged husband Jimmy, who had been an old *Northern Whig* hand, also worked for the *Newsletter*, which sometimes made life for their colleagues slightly embarrassing. Once, Jimmy Kennedy and Ralph Bossence set up a unique record for perseverance: they walked from Belfast to Dunmurry, calling at every pub along the way.

Kay Kennedy had an impeccable training for journalism. During the Second World War, known as the Emergency in the South, she worked as a shorthand typist for Cadburys in Dublin, perfecting those skills essential for journalism. After the war, she married Jimmy Kennedy and they set up home in Belfast. John Trew, who was features editor of the *Newsletter* in the early 1970s, and later became editor for seven years, remembers the extraordinary skills of Kay Kennedy in turning out fast, accurate copy. On one famous occasion, he recalls, the call came in at 2.30 one afternoon to put together a bridal supplement for the *Newsletter*. A total of 8,000 words of copy were required in three hours' time; Kay Kennedy had them ready on time, ready for typesetting and had also organised the photographs from the files.

The Duke of York was the setting for stories as numerous as the numbers of journalists who frequented it. "Bud" Bossence left enough money for his wake there; the event was unannounced, but it drew a capacity crowd who enjoyed his posthumous hospitality, in similar vein to the wake of Irish writer and journalist Brian Inglis in London early in 1993. One of the best stories about the Duke of York comes from Colin McClelland, working on the *Sunday News* in the early 1970s and now editor of the *Sunday World* in Dublin. Someone in the pub had spotted a suspicious-looking package in a doorway; in the rush to evacuate the premises, everyone inside had to step over the box, which turned out to be a hoax.

Jimmy Keaveney, who ran the family-owned pub, was the last to leave, remembers Colin McClelland. The publican stopped to collect a beer glass full of unpaid IOUs and bounced cheques, some signed by well-known people, such as Louis MacNeice, the poet. McClelland asked Keaveney why he was so keen to save this unseemingly useless collection of paper. Back shot the reply: "It's the only thing in the pub for which I would get no compo [compensation]!"

The Troubles had a much grimmer side; John Trew remembers all too vividly a number of major incidents involving fatalities in the Lower Donegall Street area in the early 1970s. On at least one occasion, sheer luck prevented the *Newsletter* offices from going up in flames. Colin McClelland says that going to work on the *Sunday News* in those harrowing days was like playing Russian roulette with the cars parked alongside the street. Still, despite the very difficult times in Belfast in the early years of the Troubles, some of the old-style newspaper characters managed to survive the coming of modern times. From the *Newsletter*, Ralph "Bud" Bossence was the most notable example, although he died in 1971.

At the *Irish News*, Tom Samways occupied that position. He was a veteran of the old hard-drinking school of journalism, brilliantly adept at his job. Born in Raglan Street in Belfast, he had joined the Belfast office of the *Daily Mail* in 1937 as a junior. He served in the Royal Navy during the Second World War and then went to work in Fleet Street, before returning to Belfast to join the *Irish News* in 1953.

He joined just in time to cover the *Princess Victoria* ferry disaster, and worked for the paper for a total of thirty-one years. During the early years of the Troubles, Samways was the night-town man on the *Irish News*, later becoming political correspondent. Once when he was down on his luck, a friend from the *Newsletter* gave him a "sub", an example of the camaraderie that has always existed among all the Belfast papers, despite surface differences. When Samways died in 1989, the *Irish News* lost one of its most colourful characters.

On the *Belfast Telegraph*, too, there were "characters", although perhaps none as daring as those who worked on the two morning newspapers. Malcolm Brodie continued his torrent of words about sport, a flow which started in earnest on *Ireland's Saturday Night* and the *Belfast Telegraph* in the early 1950s. The nearest the paper came to a real Belfast character was Fred Gamble, creator of the "John Pepper" column. One of the paper's younger reporters, Des Morrow, motoring correspondent, died young in a 1972 car crash.

But while the old-time characters still plied their stories over whiskey and stout in the Duke of York and McGlades, the editors were changing. At the *Belfast Telegraph* during the 1960s, the editor was the dour, unsmiling John Sayers; in 1969 Eugene Wasson was made editor, and the paper began to reflect more consciously the needs of the two Northern communities. This cross-community spirit, an editorial evenhandedness, continues to this day, first under Roy Lilley, editor for a long stretch from

1974 to 1991, and since then by Edmund Curran.

At the *Newsletter*, the avuncular Cowan Watson was editor, while at the *Irish News*, Terence O'Keeffe, editor of its *Irish Weekly* from 1935 to 1966, transferred to the editor's chair on the *Irish News*. He held that position until 1980, when Ted Gallagher, who had returned to Belfast and the paper where he started after a long career in the South editing the *Kerryman* and also *An Cosantoir*, the defence forces' magazine, came on board. O'Keeffe made many changes to the *Irish News*, not least improving its sports coverage. He also made the paper markedly less "Catholic" in the confessional sense and more liberal. Under his regime, three young hopefuls were eager and active: a young poet called Seamus Heaney, who contributed poetry to the paper, Paul Clarke, later to win his spurs at the BBC, and Conor O'Clery, now the Washington correspondent for *The Irish Times* and formerly that paper's first Moscow correspondent.

The transformation of the *Irish News* continued in the 1980s, under editors Martin O'Brien and then Nick Garbutt. For its centenary in 1991, the paper was substantially redesigned. In recent years, too, the paper, in common with the three Belfast newspaper groups, has invested in new printing technology, with the *Belfast Telegraph* putting in the most, around twenty million pounds. The *Newsletter*, re-equipped and now controlled by Ray Tindle, chairman, and John Barrons, chief executive, has moved from Lower Donegall Street to new premises at Boucher Road in south Belfast.

But back in the early 1970s, the most daring Belfast newspaper enterprise was the *Sunday News*, then still a lusty adolescent. Colin McClelland worked there as a young reporter. McClelland's professional upbringing had been in the world of showbiz and he recalls that Campbell often sent him on assignments for the *Sunday News* to the worst areas of the city he could think of. Later, roles were reversed, as so often happens in the newspaper business. McClelland is now the boss.

Jim Campbell is now Northern bureau chief for the *Sunday World*, working under Colin McClelland. The first editor of the *Sunday News*, Pat Carville, came from the *Irish News,* and McClelland remembers that in his time there, the *Sunday News* had one of the best newspaper production teams in the North. Its collection of columnists was eclectic and frequently controversial, people like John D. Stewart, who was often to be found in Nancy's Bar in Ardara, County Donegal, rather than at

Paper Tigers

Ralph ("Bud") Bossence, *Newsletter* columnist until his death in 1971.

Captain O. W. J. Henderson pictured when he was at the helm of Century Newspapers, then publishing the *Newsletter* and the *Sunday News*.

Malcolm Brodie, for years sports editor of the *Belfast Telegraph*, who began writing his weekly column for *Ireland's Saturday Night* in 1953.

Kay Kennedy, for long a journalist with the *Newsletter*, who died in 1993.

Eugene Wasson, editor of the *Belfast Telegraph*, 1969-74.

home in Belfast, and Patrick Riddell.

The paper was flying, as Andy Barclay recalls. He was the chief sub-editor of the *Sunday News,* and subsequently he has had a distinguished career in newspaper design in Dublin, including a long spell at the *Sunday Tribune.* He is now design editor of *The Irish Times.* He recalled recently that in the early 1970s, with riots, gunfire and "action" up and down Belfast, the *Sunday News* had editions for the upper, mid and lower Falls and the same for Shankill.

"For some readers, it was a bit like 'Spot the Ball': find your face and your friends in a fiery, frenzied photograph." The paper itself in the early 1970s was lively and campaigning, and its readership reflected exactly the 60:40 Protestant-Catholic split in Northern Ireland. In the *Newsletter,* recalled Barclay, it was always "Londonderry", while on the *Sunday News* it was "Derry". Andy Barclay also remembered the spirit of ecumenism in the paper. A death notice came in from the Foyle; a sub-editor crossed out "London". A posse of printers, readers and overseers came up; it had always been "Londonderry" and the deceased had been a member of an Orange lodge. That night Stroke City got its full appellation.

Putting the paper to bed on Saturdays was usually super-charged fun, recalls Colin McClelland, helped by such personalities as Colin McAlpine, sports editor and American Civil War enthusiast. Against all the rules, drink was brought into the office, and one or two individuals demonstrated an enormous capacity for alcohol, dashing down ouzo, beers, wines, anything that was going, their work unaffected by their liquid intake. The fun came to an end, as it always does in the newspaper industry. First of all, the *Sunday World* built up a huge Northern circulation of around 100,000, then in 1988 the *Belfast Telegraph* launched the tabloid *Sunday Life,* which became a huge success. From sales of over 100,000 a week in the 1970s, the *Sunday News* dropped to less than 25,000 copies a week in 1993, the year it closed.

The journalistic action in Belfast was not confined to these locally published papers. In the early 1970s, when the Manchester offices of the UK national newspapers were still thriving, Belfast itself thrived as an offshoot of those north of England offices. Local people worked in Belfast for the UK national papers, people like Colin Brady on the *Daily Telegraph* and his brother Robert, who ran the Belfast bureau of the *Daily Express.* The galaxy of talent included Ted Scallan on the *Daily Mail* and Joe Gorrod on the *Daily Mirror*, and photographers on that latter paper included Cyril Cain and Stanley Matchett.

John Trew remembers how in his student days at Queen's University in the early 1960s he was often paid twenty-five or thirty pounds a month for his feature ideas in the *Daily Express*. At the age of twenty-one, he was a columnist on the *Daily Express* Irish editions, writing "Go Go Go Ireland" by Johnny Robb. That carefree newspaper spirit in Belfast persisted right into the 1970s, aided by the likes of Henry Kelly, who was covering the North for *The Irish Times* when the Troubles were starting, and who had some narrow escapes, leavened by subsequent humour, just like Colin Brady and indeed most journalists of the time.

Vincent Browne, now editor of the *Sunday Tribune*, Dublin, was involved in a famous escapade when he was working for the *Irish Press* in Belfast. He presented a gun - said to have been made at a loyalist engineering works in the city - at a press conference in what was then the Europa Hotel, later the Forum. A posse of security personnel met him, including, it is said, forty-three representatives from the RUC. Browne was lucky to escape the mandatory jail sentence for carrying weapons, and even though he was subsequently fined twenty pounds, he got a terrific story in the best Vincent Browne tradition.

A Belfast newspaper character from an earlier era made his last working appearances at the start of the Troubles. During the late 1930s and into the first years of the Second World War, Seaghan Maynes, brought up on the Falls Road and educated at St Malachy's College, was the best-known reporter on the *Irish News* and had many news scoops.

Once during the war, he was standing in a Belfast phone box dictating copy to the office, only to be dragged out by an RUC man. Seconds later, what Maynes thought had been a bailed-out German airman turned out to be a parachute mine, which hit the box. Maynes joined Reuters news agency in 1943. His career there included seven years as White House correspondent and ended with him returning home to Belfast to cover the Troubles in the early 1970s.

By the middle of that decade, in Colin McClelland's remembrance, the party was starting to run out of time. At its height, local and visiting journalists covered frightful atrocities and swapped yarns in the journalistic hostelries. If anyone went into McGlades and found the place empty, it was a tell-tale sign that a big story had broken. The spirit of the age was typified by the weekly press conferences held late every Monday morning at the Wellington Park Hotel on the Malone Road by Gordon Duffield (once of the *Belfast Telegraph*, then in at the start of Ulster Television in 1959) who subsequently set up his own public relations company. Duffield and his assistant, Robin Dunseith, attracted many Belfast media personalities with their amiable and relaxed hospitality, including the Rosenfield sisters, Ray and Judith, Cathal McCabe, now head of music in RTE, and Ronnie Hoffmann, then of the *Newsletter*, who subsequently went to work for *The Irish Times* in Belfast and then in Dublin before going out to the Australian newspaper industry in Melbourne.

Then as the international media started getting bored with the Northern Troubles, they began to drift away. Eventually, numbers of Belfast journalists did the same, including Ray Managh to Independent Newspapers in Dublin, Ken Reid to the *Cork Examiner*, Colin McClelland to the *Sunday World*. McClelland says that Captain Bill Henderson, the *Newsletter* mastermind, said to him rather plaintively, when he announced he was going to work in Dublin, "You'll be back." He wasn't, the party was over, and although the Belfast newspaper scene has changed dramatically over the last twenty years, computerised, more business-like, perhaps the fun isn't what it was in the early 1970s – that heady mixture of fear, frolics and old-time journalistic japes.

Chapter 9

The Gossip Columnists

• • •

Gossip columns are one of the expanding areas of modern Irish newspapers, relating tittle-tattle about socialites and stories about the great and the infamous. Terry Keane, whose column appears in the *Sunday Independent*, relates one unpleasant experience in her work.

"I think my greatest nightmare was having lunch with Jerry Hall, the model and wife of Mick Jagger; I found her one of the least interesting people I have ever met. Trying to write it up afterwards was probably the most difficult thing I ever had to do. A lot of people are very much nicer than you would assume before you meet them. Of course, you do meet the bitches or the male equivalent, whatever that is, who turn out to be rather nasty. I met one couple who had separated and were both very successful in their own right. I had lunch with him and I thought he was the most ghastly man I had ever met and about five months later I met his wife or ex-wife. I thought, I am bound to like her because he is so horrible and they have split up, but she was equally terrible. There are no hard and fast rules."

Terry Keane's weekly back-page column is required reading for what it does not say as much as for what it does. Gossip columns are one of the growth areas of present-day Irish journalism, although the people who write them prefer to be called by the more respectable title of social columnists. It is also the one area of journalism where women predominate, as Myles McWeeney of the *Irish Independent* explains.

"I think there are only one or two of us males in the preserve, including Trevor Danker of the *Sunday Independent*; it makes for some amusing exchanges with one's colleagues because quite often if I have to go to a Paul Costelloe showing - or those of other designers - my comments,

Tom Hennigan, ever the jaunty journalist, rides a penny farthing bicycle down Middle Abbey Street in Dublin, outside the *Evening Herald* offices, for a promotion. He wrote the nightly social diary on the paper and was as well known as Terry O'Sullivan at many social events in the 1960s. He started his career, as did so many other noted journalists, on the *Western People* in Ballina.

Right: Patsy Dyke, who wrote for the old *Sunday Review* and then for the *Sunday Press*.

Left: Terry Keane, controversial back-page columnist for the *Sunday Independent*.

which are usually rather frank and honest about the prices of these garments, sometimes wind up in the women writers' columns."

So how do people step into this sybaritic style of journalism? Myles McWeeney tells of his extensive family background in journalism. "My great-grandfather was a journalist with the *Freeman's Journal*. He was editor, which was then called chief reporter. Both my father and two of my uncles were journalists and my mother was a journalist. But my Uncle Cecil - Cecil McWeeney - was founding editor of *Social & Personal* magazine when it came out in the late 1930s and he continued editing it until his death. He always used to say he never had to buy lunch for himself."

Barbara McKeon writes the daily social column on the *Irish Press* and explains how she was propelled into the job. "Well, actually it happened a couple of years ago when the *Irish Press* group was in a little bit of trouble and was almost going to the wall. The then diarist, Michael Sheridan, had left and the job was passed around. I was doing a television column at the time and I honestly think they gave me the job because if I made a complete cock up of it, nobody would notice. But then the paper survived and they were so surprised that I had done rather well that they offered me the job permanently. I was delighted to take it on."

The whole business of publishing social columns only really started in Irish newspapers in the 1960s. One of the first and certainly one of the widely read columnists at the time was Patsy Dyke of the *Sunday Press* who came into it entirely by chance.

"I went into *The Irish Times* newsroom to collect my husband, Cathal O'Shannon, and John Healy and Douglas Gageby were sitting over in the corner. John had the idea that he wanted a girl to do the social column in the *Sunday Review*. I just walked in and they said, 'There she is', and I didn't know what they were talking about. But I was delighted. I had started my life on a magazine called *Country Life*, which was far removed from social columns, but I thought why not give it a go and I did. Well, it started just as a Saturday night diary and I had to go around and get into hotels, twenty-first birthday parties, weddings, and if there were any names in town or any personalities, to cover them as well. It developed into two diaries, with one for the country. John had this idea that it should be upmarket, so I had a lovely Mercedes car to travel around in and I was told to stay in the best hotels. That was really tough!"

The *Sunday Review* folded at the end of 1963. Then Patsy Dyke got a summons from Conor O'Brien, then editor of the *Evening Press*, to go and see Major Vivion de Valera. "I was a little worried because only a week before I had been at a party and danced with him and I hadn't thought very much of his dancing, so I wondered what he was going to say to me. But he did ask me whether I would like a job and I thought that was wonderful. So they asked me if I would do the same sort of thing on the *Sunday Press*, two diaries a week, one for the country and one on Saturday night. But he warned me, 'I don't want any sort of bitchiness or any malice, it is too easy to do that sort of thing. If you don't like the people or the subject that you are covering, just leave it out. That's the worst thing that could happen to them.'"

The 1960s was a good time to be alive and working in Ireland. The country was bursting with a new spirit, as Patsy Dyke remembers. "It was a very exciting time to be going around Ireland. We had the idea that we wanted to include, for want of a better word, ordinary people, and the ordinary people in those days were really getting up and going places. We met people who were organising festivals, not just the Rose of Tralee or the Galway Oyster Festival, small festivals to coincide with emigrants coming home in August and things like that - Mary of Dungloe and Drumshanbo's An Tostal, the longest running festival of all."

But writing a social column has always needed bags of energy. Barbara McKeon reveals her recipe. "A sense of humour and a good wardrobe. You need to keep going - always like having a good time and keep a good head, especially in the morning after a very late night."

Patsy Dyke recalls one of her most gruelling assignments and also some of the perks. "In those days I had a good capacity to drink alcohol late into the night and sometimes it meant you were drinking in the priest's house. In Athlone it was a friend of my husband's, the commandant of the local barracks, and it was also Paddy Lenihan, the man from Kilfenora, and Brian's daddy. These two gentlemen took me in hand and for two days we sampled the delights of Athlone, the Hodson Bay Hotel and everywhere around Athlone and I suddenly remembered that one of the things I had to do in those two days was to interview John Broderick, the wonderful author who also was a baker in Athlone. By the time I got to him I was really so hungover and John was so sympathetic towards this condition that we actually did get a good interview out of him, so Athlone is still one of my favourite places. We also met people like John Huston, the film director, who was living down in Galway.

"I met Grace Kelly and I was invited over to Monaco and interviewed her in the palace. I went to all sorts of lovely homes, hunt balls. I saw Sonia Ffrench down twenty dozen oysters at the Galway Oyster Festival, which I thought was some feat. I interviewed Lady Astor who at seventy-nine was still riding side-saddle, and of course Molly Cusack Smith, who thankfully is still with us, gave one of the best hunt balls in north Galway. So I think it is still going on, but I would rather read about it now than write about it."

Barbara McKeon finds her work style a good way of stretching her salary. "From my point of view, I enjoy the travel. I enjoy little things. I was at Clarinbridge for the Oyster Festival, and they laid on a stretch limousine for us to go anywhere we wanted. It was wonderful being chauffeur-driven. We went off, about four of us, for a drink in Kinvara. We pulled up outside a pub in the stretch limousine, which took up half the village, and deposited ourselves inside and had a couple of whiskies and it was very enjoyable. Then you can go abroad - I have been in the south of France and Morocco and they are very pleasant, I must say. I will tell you what the best part is - it does actually afford a lifestyle that is extremely expensive and indeed on a journalist's salary impossible to keep up. It means that I am having a lifestyle that is beyond my means, but is not costing me too much money at all."

Terry Keane, a doyenne of the drawing-room set, rather enjoys it all and has her favourite places. "I do normal things as well and obviously nobody wants to read about me going shopping to supermarkets so I write about the brighter side but I mean I have a fairly balanced life, just like anybody else. It is only a job which happens to reflect part of my lifestyle, that is all. So I don't think the socialising is particularly hard work and if it was, I wouldn't do it. I enjoy meeting people and I enjoy going out to dinner, enjoy my friends, enjoy parties. I love travelling. I don't find that a burden and I rather like writing about it."

She has choice locations in Ireland and abroad. "It's no secret that I adore being in Kerry, my favourite part of Ireland, and I have just come back from Paris; I have to say it is hard to beat."

Putting a column together, whether day by day or from Sunday to Sunday, is hard work. Terry Keane, Myles McWeeney and Barbara

McKeon give a glimpse of the slog behind the glitz and the glamour. "Deadlines, like in everybody's job - deadlines. It's very difficult to convince people that it is our job because there are so many wonderful events at which you get to meet fascinating people: the artists, the writers, the people who are movers and shakers. You get to travel and you imbibe the finest champagnes and wines and dine in restaurants and hotels and it is very difficult to explain to people that sometimes I want to pull my hair out by its dyed roots and run screaming into a sanatorium", says Barbara McKeon.

"I do the column four days a week, on a Tuesday, Wednesday, Thursday and Friday, and it is probably between 800 and 1,000 words a day but that would be broken down into four or five stories. The real skill in being a columnist is to be able to distill a lot of information into a very short space", adds Myles McWeeney. Terry Keane talks about covering a recent artistic event: "I did the Edward Maguire retrospective exhibition and I decided just to write about people who were there with their second wives or second husbands, which puts a different slant on it to just giving a list of people."

Being a columnist means meeting with top people; sometimes a tip from them can pay off, as Barbara McKeon reveals: "I was at the races in Leopardstown, it was a beautiful, glorious summer's day and I saw the Aga Khan. I approached him and said, 'Ah, your Highness, how are you, would you have a tip for the next race?' His minders were eyeing me cautiously and he said, 'Well, you could do worse than put your money on my horse in the next race', which I did and I made a modest amount and it added to a very pleasant day. Going home that evening, having been deposited in St Stephen's Green, I was going for a taxi and I thought I might as well use my ill-gotten gains to my advantage, so I hailed a horse-drawn carriage and imperiously ordered it to take me to Ranelagh. It cost me considerably more than a taxi but it was well worth the ride."

Terry Keane enjoyed spending a couple of days with Joan Collins, the actress. "I thought she was a very down-to-earth, amusing woman, very practical, totally unlike her image." Sometimes the public remembers kindly, as Patsy Dyke found out. "In Limerick recently a man came up to me and I must say I thought at first he was going to snatch my handbag, but really he wanted to say, 'Thank you very much for writing that nice piece about me in 1967.' I thought, my goodness, there are still a few fans alive."

"Well, I suppose I am part of it, aren't I? That great tapestry of bitchery in Dublin, the daily spite of that unmannerly town, but I try not to be spiteful. I don't think I am spiteful and it is certainly not written in a spiteful way. It is more written in a satirical and, I hope, an amusing way", adds Terry Keane.

Chapter 10

Smokey Joe and the Munster Express

· · ·

J.J. WALSH, FOR MANY years owner and editor of the *Munster Express* in Waterford, was a legend in his own lifetime and the source of many anecdotes, many deriving from his powerful personality and numerous achievements. He died in September 1992. Frank Hall, a veteran of the provincial newspaper scene, with such RTE programmes as "Hall's Pictorial Weekly", recalls what was said about J. J. Walsh, popularly known as Smokey Joe, in the aftermath of his death.

"Tramore Town Commissioners paid tribute to the memory of the late J. J. Walsh, Chairman of the *Munster Express*. Commissioner Chairman Mr Sean Brennan proposed a vote of sympathy at Tuesday night's monthly meeting and referred to Mr Walsh as a controversial figure who had glorified in that image. He said there were so many anecdotes about him that they would be told for years to come. The most fortunate thing about him was that he had a long and fruitful life and that at the end of his days he had his family to look after him. All the other members associated themselves with the comments."

Kieran Walsh, one of his sons, is now managing director, running the paper which is among Ireland's oldest provincials. "My father died on 10 September at 6.00 am in Dublin, following a fairly long illness. He had been very active in the business up to twelve months ago previously, when he was eighty-five-years old. He had a major influence in Waterford City for forty to fifty years. His enormous persona is sadly missed in the city and throughout the country, especially for those in the publishing and printing business. Myself, I have been involved in the newspaper since 1984. My sister Priscilla has been involved in the paper since the late 1970s and she has an influence presently. My late mother, Josephine, also had an interest in the paper and my brother Edward assists in putting together copy for the paper. It has been in the Walsh family since the early 1900s. There was another paper which belonged to a relative, called the *Waterford Citizen,* and my grandfather acquired this title from a relative and in the same year he also acquired the *Munster Express*. He merged the two titles within the year and decided that the *Munster Express* had a better ring to it and moved premises from the *Waterford Citizen* to our present premises on the Quay."

J. J. Walsh took over the running of the paper from his father, Edward, who also had been a big shot in Waterford – mayor as well as owner and editor. At one time at the turn of the century, Waterford had more than half a dozen main papers. Now the honours are shared between the *Munster Express* and the *Waterford News & Star,* which is owned by the *Cork Examiner*. But for the last forty or fifty years, the newspaper talk in Waterford has always centered on the doings of J. J. Walsh, the source of many wonderful anecdotes, the man who even wrote his own obituary. No one knows quite how he got his famous nickname but John O'Connor on the reporting staff of the paper revealed something close to the truth about two more legends surrounding Smokey Joe.

"A lot of his contemporaries have gone, so many people who thought they knew him actually didn't know him and the J. J. Walsh they knew is the J. J. Walsh of the anecdotes and the stories. In fact, most of the stories about him that did the rounds weren't true at all. The really good ones I doubt will ever cross the four walls of the *Munster Express*. There were popular ones which weren't true, I suppose one of the more famous ones being the one about the salt cellar. Mr Walsh wore a toupée and people would swear that before he entered the room he had a little salt cellar in his pocket, which he would sprinkle on his shoulders to feign dandruff. It was a great yarn but it just wasn't true. And the other one was the famous story about the blacklist in the *Munster Express*. You would meet people who would say, 'Well, you will never see me in the *Munster Express*' because of some slight or other. Ninety-nine per cent of the time the boss hadn't even heard of the people concerned and there was certainly no blacklist. I think over all the years there were a couple of people he wasn't particularly fond of, but you would count them on the fingers of one hand."

Michael Whelan, former advertisement manager of the *Munster Express*.

J. J. Walsh climbing the Great Wall of China; he was on his way home from the Seoul Olympics in 1988.

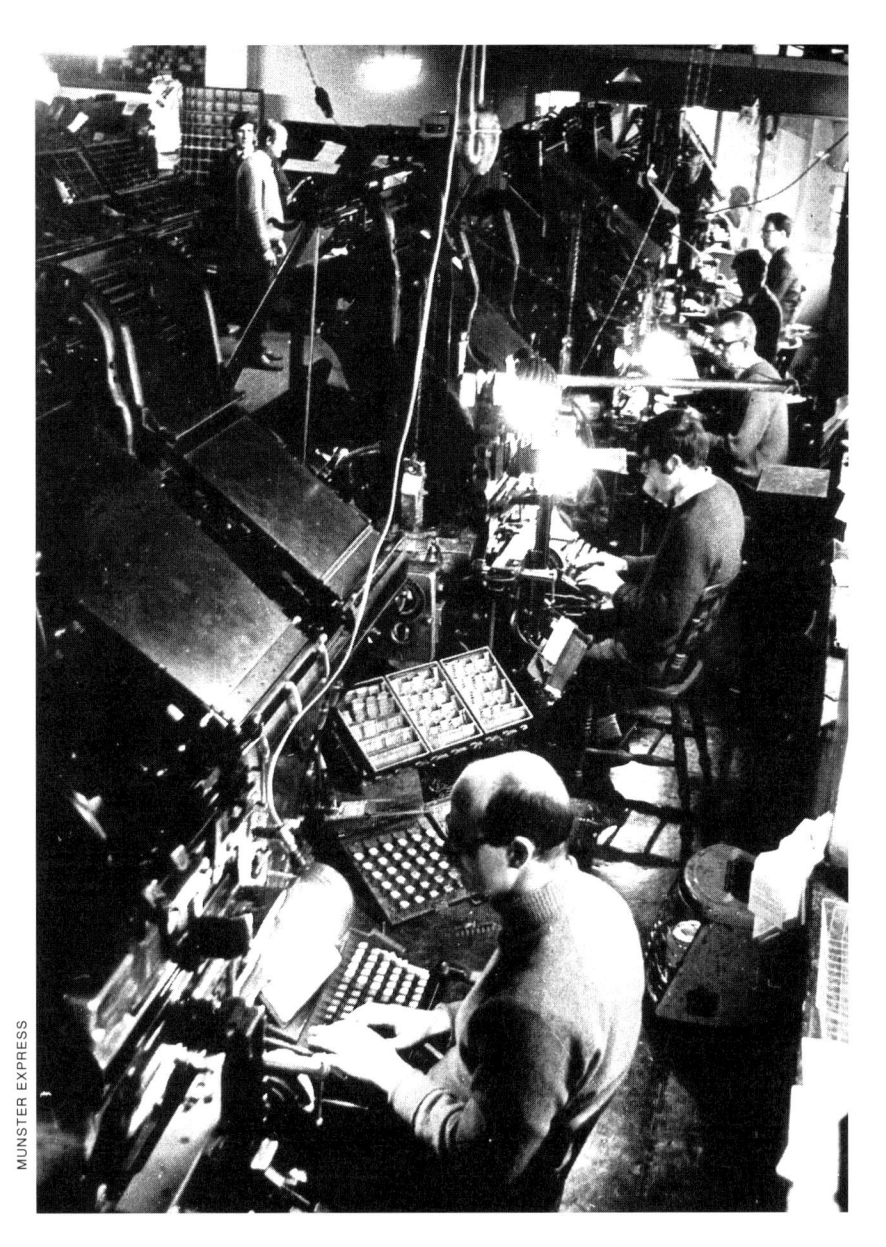

Linotype hot metal setting in the *Munster Express*, Waterford.

The old-fashioned front office of the *Munster Express*, as seen in 1992, with its pine panelling and holy pictures, looks caught in a time warp, but it belies the many technical and editorial advances made at the paper under its wealthy owner. There were other sides to J. J. Walsh's character, too. When he was younger, he invented some ingenious printing devices and throughout his life he contributed much to Waterford charities. His retired advertisement manager and deputy chief executive Michael Whelan looks back on his boss with affection.

"Well, we always referred to him as the Chief. The Chief was always the type of person who in an emergency was one of the very first to take off his coat and pitch in with the rest of the staff. Nowadays, that is just not done."

"We don't have messenger boys any more, but I remember when we did have messenger boys here, if J. J. was up the town and met one of them, he would make a great show of talking to him. He was a proud man, but he hadn't a snobbish bone in his body, which I think is a very good thing to say about him. He treated everybody equally and I think that was one of his great traits", adds John O'Connor.

For everyone working at the *Munster Express*, life was always lively, rarely predictable and never dull, as John O'Connor continues: "For J. J. Walsh, the duty of a newspaper was to shake things up. He would be horrified if somebody tried to portray him as a saint. He wasn't and wouldn't wish to be thought as such. He was like everybody else, he had his moments. There were often times when he was unreasonable and he had a great habit of raising his voice. A lot of his staff acquired the same habit and very often, especially on press days, during summer times, you would often see people looking up at the open windows in amazement, as the sound of battle drifted down to the street. But overall, I would say he treated people fairly and if you did your job and did what was expected of you, there was no problem."

The rows on the paper were often volcanic in their splendour, and sometimes dragged on. "They weren't that shortlived; they could last a few days, even a week, and I often suspected that when things were too quiet, Mr Walsh would start a few rows to jizz things up a bit. He thrived on argument and there was nothing better when things stirred under him. In a way he had a point; some of the weeks here, when there were screams, roars and arguments from one department to the other, the end result was a particularly good newspaper."

But still the stories and legends persist about Smokey Joe. Rich fables were created, layer upon layer. John O'Connor remembers. "Well, I suppose one of the famous ones was the one about the negotiations for machine extras, very recently. There had been negotiations about machine extras for the press. Mr Walsh introduced the 'talks about talks' idea long before it was ever heard of in Northern Ireland, getting an agenda going, strand one and two, all of twenty years ago. He operated along that kind of line, but the talks were getting nowhere. In the end, anyway, Mr Walsh said to the lads: 'Look, I think that I could get a couple of monkeys to do what I want ye to do', and the lads retorted, 'Well, okay, go ahead and get a couple of monkeys.' So he got up from the chair, he had to have the last word. He just got to the door, opened it and looked back and said, 'I would, only ye would make them join the union.'"

Smokey Joe nearly made the wider stage. Nearly fifty years ago, there seemed a good chance he would be elected to the Dáil and be made Minister for Education. Then in the 1950s, the Murphy family, who then owned Independent Newspapers in Dublin, wanted him to become chief executive. He declined, preferring Waterford, his native city.

He had a keen interest in history, having always believed that Waterford should portray itself in a positive way, that we should learn from the past and build for the future. He was Life President of the Waterford Literary and Historical Society and he was also involved with the Military History Society and wrote a book, *Waterford's Yesterdays and Tomorrows*. He would nearly know every family on particular streets in Waterford, such was his detailed knowledge of the city and its buildings.

J. J. Walsh's late widow, Josephine, recalled some of her husband's leisure interests. "He enjoyed travelling and golf; he would go to Spain twice a year to play golf. He worked hard and travelled and enjoyed himself."

He also kept racehorses, insisting on them being run in the town where he had his big residence, Tramore, as Kieran Walsh recalls: "A lot of people were happy with J. J.'s horses because they never really failed during the early days, although he had one horse that didn't do so well. Generally they came out on top."

A perceptive *Cork Examiner* columnist, Sean Dunne, grew up in Waterford and he wrote recently that when he was a boy it seemed as if

Smokey Joe had photographed every building in the world for the *Munster Express*. When he was eighty-two-years old, Smokey Joe himself was pictured climbing up the Great Wall of China, a huge grin on his face as if he had just bought the whole lot. That trip which took in the Seoul Olympics in Korea in 1988 was his last visit to the Olympic Games. He had been to all of them since Berlin in 1936 and John O'Connor has a yarn about that one.

"Well, it was again part of his sense of humour that when Jesse Owens, the great black American athlete, died somebody in RTE decided that they wanted a different angle. They decided to ring Mr Walsh because he had been at every Olympics since Berlin; they asked him did he remember Jesse Owens? The famous story is that when Jesse Owens won his fourth gold medal, Hitler was so enraged that he turned his back and stormed out of the stadium. There is an historical doubt about whether that actually happened, but anyway when the interviewer asked Mr Walsh, he said, 'Oh, yes, when Jesse won his last gold medal, I went over and shook him by the hand and congratulated him. Whatever way I looked up, I saw Adolph [Hitler] and he looked down and he turned his back on Jesse and myself and stormed out of the stadium.'

"There was another story about him, just to tell you how conservative he was in ways. He was a great admirer of Franco and made no secret of it. In 1975, when it became known that Franco was ill and death was imminent, he marched down the Quay into Harvey's travel office and across a crowded room told the managing director: 'As soon as you hear Franco is dead, book me straight through to the funeral', and he went to the funeral. I think he was the only Irish newspaper editor at Franco's funeral."

The summing up of the last of his kind in the newspaper business is left to Frank Hall and Michael Whelan. "His presence is still in the *Munster Express*. I am sure that the staff would often look over their shoulders to see if he was coming in the door. They felt that he was there all the time and that he was guiding them and I am sure that the atmosphere still is here in the office, that he is with us and he is telling them what to do, how it should be done. The *Munster Express* continues to work like a well-oiled machine.

"In Waterford he was venerated, an extraordinary man; he could be talking to a titled person and five minutes afterwards, he could be talking to a person who was on the rocks and had better times. He gave the same treatment to that person as he did to the titled person", concludes Michael Whelan.

"I knew him purely in the social way and on that level he was a most pleasant, affable and a very nice man. It was always a pleasure to meet him and there was always a bit of fun and laughter when you were talking to him. But I was thinking how strange it is that now all his anecdotes are coming out; now he is being assessed and reassessed and it is becoming plain only now, I think, to most people that he was a quite remarkable person as a publisher and as a journalist. It seems to me, and I don't think it too fanciful, that he should be compared with people like Lord Beaverbrook and Lord Northcliffe; even at that end of the scale, that kind of 'robber baron' journalist and owner no longer exists. They were a law unto themselves, and they regarded their newspapers as an extension of their own personality", was Frank Hall's estimation.

"We've often heard that it's the end of an era and we will never look upon the likes of J. J. Walsh again, and that's a bit hackneyed. But at the same time one would rather reluctantly have to say that it is probably true", he concludes.

Chapter 11

The Sunday Newspapers

• • •

NO SECTOR OF THE IRISH newspaper market is more competitive than Sunday newspapers. The five Dublin-published titles compete ferociously with each other and the huge influx of UK titles. The *News of the World* alone sells more copies in Ireland than the *Irish Independent* does on a normal day. Columnists figure frequently, and Hugh Leonard, who is a regular contributor to the *Sunday Independent*, remembers one amusing incident.

"I think one of the funniest things that happened to me which I included in a column was when I had a rodent ulcer which had to be surgically removed; it was at the corner of my eye and it was a very small operation, as a result of which I had this enormous discolouration on the eye. I had to go out to lunch soon afterwards and Mr Haughey, whom I had never met really, was sitting in the restaurant with a bunch of his cronies. Brian Lenihan got up to say hello and I talked to him. As I headed for the stairs, I could hear the inimitable voice of C. J. H. saying, 'I see that somebody has given the blankety blank blank a black eye at last.'"

Competition among Sunday newspapers is absolutely cut-throat, as Aengus Fanning, editor of the *Sunday Independent*, makes very clear. He comes from a long newspaper tradition; his family are the Fannings of *Midland Tribune* fame from Birr, County Offaly. Yet in recalling the long service of a former *Sunday Independent* editor, Hector Legge, he describes how once the paper had the field to itself.

"Hector was a brilliant and astute editor whom I think was the longest serving editor in Irish newspapers: thirty years and two weeks, he never fails to remind me. But after all, through most of that time, there were basically only two Irish Sunday titles on the market. In fact, at one time there weren't even two because the *Sunday Press* hadn't been started."

When the *Sunday Press* was launched in 1949 by Sean Lemass it was revolutionary. Michael Keane, present *Sunday Press* editor, details the novel and intricate way in which circulation was built up.

"One of the main reasons why the *Sunday Press* was so successful is that it set out to be outside every single first Mass in the country in Cahirciveen, County Kerry, as well as Carndonagh, County Donegal, which was no mean achievement in 1949. Since first Mass was quite often at 7.00 am, that was some target. The late Padraig Ó Criogain [Paddy Creegan], who died in 1992, then circulation manager, helped to bring on the parent paper the *Irish Press* and he went at it with military precision. They were outside Mass every Sunday morning and helped to capture quite a large sale, to such an extent that in the late 1950s circulation had risen to over 350,000.

"Lieutenant Colonel Matt Feehan was the first editor of the *Sunday Press* and he ran it with an iron discipline. He was very successful and very strong on articles like the Dan Breen story, that type of thing, and how the ambushes in the Civil War were carried out, and the great victories. But he also was very, very meticulous in terms of news, and concentrated on news while the opposition possibly didn't so much. He was succeeded by Francis Carty, known as the 'little man'. Frank was a meticulous journalist and very highly regarded in his own right. Then Vincent Jennings came from the *Evening Press* and was, I think, nineteen years as editor here. He began to transform and change the paper and bring it more up to date with a lot of competition, and in an era when the *Sunday World* began to come on the market and you had television coming into its heyday. You had tremendous amount of competition from the British press but you also had the development of the *Sunday Tribune* and the *Sunday Independent*. The latter paper had been rambling along, but began to be much more vibrant. In Christmas 1986 Vincent became chief executive of the company and I succeeded him. I had been brought in as deputy editor three years before that."

Since the 1960s, the market has become much more competitive, but Aengus Fanning says that the sales of the *Sunday Independent* continued to climb even in the midst of the recent recession. He explains his editorial policy.

"We have writers of the calibre of Anthony Cronin, Ronan Fanning,

John A. Murphy, and we have entertaining dimensions like Terry Keane, Declan Lynch and Barry Egan. Most people know that Sam Smyth broke the Greencore story in the *Sunday Independent* and set in motion a train of events that I suppose you could say led eventually to a change of government. One gets complaints from sports fans about Eamon Dunphy or Mick Doyle and one gets complaints that Terry Keane is over the top, but basically her personality is consciously over the top. It entertains people and I always say if I can get a laugh out of a reader, it's worth 2,000 words."

There is also a cosy little family arrangement on the paper with Terry Keane and her daughter Madeleine. "My daughter Madeleine is working on the *Sunday Independent*. She is on what I should say the 'more respectable side'. She does book reviews, theatre interviews and pieces like that; she's not on the seamier side of the paper!"

Writing a Sunday column has its own pains and pleasures. Hugh Leonard finds, week in week out, that he has problems and difficulties discovering new people to write about. "Well, the only problem is that I am running out of *bêtes noires*. Ulick [O'Connor] is keeping his head down a lot. Charlie [Haughey] is gone now and I have to find a few more people to castigate. I haven't heard about Sean Doherty in a long time now so I have to cast around a bit and find new ones. People like to see other people being pulled off their high horses and I enjoy doing it when I can. It adds a little bit of flavour to the column, I think."

But in Dalkey, County Dublin, where he lives he has made one restaurateur, Mervyn Stewart, a happy man. "I was telling you earlier that Mervyn runs a restaurant here called the Guinea Pig, a very good restaurant, and I said a few kind words about him. Later I was told that Mervyn was wearing his hat and smoking a cheroot, and I asked what does that mean and they said, 'Whenever anybody praises Mervyn, he stands at the door of his shop and he wears a hat and he smokes a cheroot.' I hadn't realised that nothing escapes notice very much in Dalkey."

The first serious new competition in the quality newspaper Sunday market came with the launch of the *Sunday Tribune* in 1980. Vincent Browne, the present editor, talks about some of his tribulations since he took over in 1983. Recently the paper has been dramatically repackaged.

"Well, the relaunch of the paper back in April 1983 was obviously the most critical development. We had a number of financial difficulties arising from the withdrawal of Tony Ryan from the project in the summer of

Hugh Leonard, *Sunday Independent* columnist.

Eamon Dunphy, another controversial *Sunday Independent* columnist.

Anne Harris, features editor of the *Sunday Independent*.

1984, and they were certainly memorable. We also had difficulties arising from the unfortunate timing of the launch of the *Dublin Tribune* in the summer of 1990. But we have now settled down, I believe, on a fairly even keel. I would have thought the most notable change is on the cover and that's the first thing one notices; we have dropped the glossily published cover and we now have a traditional front page. We had wanted to do this back in 1988 and 1989 long before we heard even of the *Sunday Business Post*'s imminent arrival. But we were unable to do it because of printing constraints; our printer couldn't have done the job that we are now able to do."

An even newer paper, the *Sunday Business Post*, is now heading into its fourth year. Its management and international investors hold the shares. Barbara Nugent, its new chief executive who arrived in the autumn of 1992, details progress to date, including some rationalisation.

"The paper is not making money and I don't think that it will be in a position where I will be able to say that until 1994, but I think after that, yes. By the very nature and size of the paper it will never be a highly profitable paper, but it certainly can be profitable and that's where we are going. There was quite a lot of rationalisation done over the last year and I think that it has put the paper on a very strong footing to consolidate and grow. It has been a tremendous help and it was quite good to come in after that had been done rather than actually to have to do it oneself. It's not the nicest thing to have to do especially when peoples' livelihoods are at stake but unfortunately one has to measure the livelihood of everybody against a few and that was done. I am confident that there is a very strong niche for the *Sunday Business Post*."

Staying on top in the Sunday newspaper battle means a constant stream of new ideas. Vincent Browne looks to the future while Aengus Fanning talks about keeping in step with that fickle creature, public opinion.

"Public opinion these days is more mature than it was fifteen years ago. I don't think there is much to be gained by continuously hanging back ten years behind the mainstream of public opinion. If you do that day in and day out, you will have a very old-fashioned sort of newspaper. One has to just push ahead a little bit; basically our readers like what we are giving them and they put their money where their liking is. It's not an exact science and one never gets it perfectly right, but I hope we are pitched in the middle of the trend", says Aengus Fanning.

The Sunday Newspapers

Barbara Nugent, chief executive of the *Sunday Business Post*.

Below: Micheal Keane, editor of the *Sunday Press*.

Francis Carty, second editor of the *Sunday Press*, and also an editor of the *Irish Press*.

Aengus Fanning, editor of the *Sunday Independent*.

"Already we are providing by far the largest volume of quality news coverage on a Sunday. What we are going to improve really are the features and lifestyle sections of the paper; that's the major deficiency I reckon we have at present. We are giving a lot of attention and concentration to that area", Vincent Browne concludes.

Michael Keane gives the philosophy behind the *Sunday Press* and charts the hopes for the future. "We are a family newspaper. We are not trying to be sensationalist; we are not trying to go for the gratuitously violent or sexual. We are trying to cater for an audience that is sophisticated but doesn't like to be offended either and we are moving stage by stage. It is not a crash programme and we hope to bring our readers with us. I think the additional resources, concentration on investigative journalism, and the addition of good political writing move good writers in general, the development of the sports area with people like Liam Hayes and feature writers like Brenda Power. We will be concentrating on building up a good team of excellent writers who can reflect the modern Ireland; we have some excellent people on the staff now and we are gearing up for further developments."

As Michael Keane says, readers are very quick to vent their likes and dislikes, much more so than in the old days. Hugh Leonard gets the same reaction to his *Sunday Independent* column.

"The good factor is that I get an extraordinary amount of feedback to the column, from people who go to places that I recommend abroad. Sometimes feedback isn't that good; once I went to Kenmare when I was writing a column called 'Not While I Am Eating', a kind of food column. A Kerryman came over and said: 'I see you are only interested in filling your gut these days.' You always walk into that kind of situation and it is always unexpected. It is the occasion of *l'ésprit d'escalier*: you think of a clever reply while you are on the bus on your way home. And I have noticed another thing, the readiness with which people nowadays want to sue for libel. Libel suits come up out of the ground whereas a couple of years ago I would never hear from a solicitor, but now the word has got around. Usually the verdict will go against the newspaper because the newspaper has a lot of money and so people quite readily go into court."

Chapter 12

The Cork Examiner

• • •

Out of all the daily papers in Ireland, the *Cork Examiner* is the oldest, founded in 1841. It and its sister paper, the *Evening Echo*, are institutions in Cork City and County and Munster, as Jack Lynch, a former Taoiseach who was born and brought up in Cork City, recalls.

"I lived near Shandon, an inner suburb, and the *Echo* covered all the local city news, but the *Examiner* was more catholic in the sense of taking the county and national news as well. So that is the reason the *Echo* was probably more popular in the houses around the fringes of the city.

"Naturally, I was a very young hurler and Gaelic footballer and I always looked out for the Gaelic news, the reports of matches in retrospect and prospects of matches to come. But for ordinary features, 'Mutt & Jeff' was the one we all looked for. It's still going and in our young days, when the *Echo* arrived, my grandmother, who was then alive, always commandeered the *Echo* because she wanted to see first of all the headings of the main items. Then, of course, she looked to see who was dead, in other words she wanted to find out if any of her old friends had passed away, and then she turned to 'Mutt & Jeff' and of course we were all looking over her shoulder as soon as she turned to the page the 'Mutt & Jeff' feature was on."

He also remembers the famous *Evening Echo* newsboys. "Ah, yes indeed, they were great, they were part of the city, part of the scene. They still are to a certain extent, but they were controlled by a legendary figure called Johnny Mahony. Johnny was known as the King of the *Echo* boys. He must have had thirty or forty of them in his employ and I think he had a great rapport with the boys and he in turn with the *Cork Examiner* because there was never any sign of blackguarding or any sign of little boys running away with the money. Johnny had great control of them and they had very great trust in him and he in them. He has gone now long since; he bought a pub in Blarney Street afterwards, but he has a brother who still operates near the cathedral in Cork called Flaherty's corner. He's still there quietly but he doesn't shout out the *Echo* as the kids used to do in the old days.

"The *Echo* cry - 'eekwah' - was wonderful. When I came to Dublin first, I heard the young fellows shouting, 'Heggald and Mail' (*Evening Herald* and *Evening Mail*), but I thought that the one for the *Echo* was a bit more melodic."

As for the *Cork Examiner* itself, it has been in continuous circulation longer than any of the Dublin dailies. The paper has also had a long history of technical firsts in the Irish newspaper industry. Ted Crosbie, chairman, details just one recent development.

"These papers are now respectively 152- and 101-years old and are taking their breath before getting into the twenty-first century. I wouldn't have believed five years ago that we could send a photographer out to Kenya and up to Somalia and that in over twelve hours we could receive twelve colour wire pictures over an ordinary telephone line. I hate to tell you what the cost of the telephone line was, but they were very good quality indeed."

Tim Cramer, who was *Cork Examiner* editor for seven years and who is now a director, literary editor and the man in charge of the various supplements each week, reflects on the 1992 *Evening Echo* centenary and the *Cork Examiner*'s patrimony.

"We had the *Echo* centenary in 1992 and produced a special *Echo* for the occasion, mostly looking back at old Cork. I think Cork people are heavily into nostalgia. In 1991 we did a very big supplement on the *Examiner* for its 150th anniversary, which I was involved in. In fact, I think it was probably the biggest job I ever undertook in here because it was largely a one-man job, it had to be. But it was fascinating to go back over all the old *Examiners* and find details of those horrendous events like the famine, which touched me very deeply. You had the whole gamut of Irish history from then on. With the Easter Rising, the *Cork Examiner* was the only newspaper to condemn the shootings of the 1916 leaders. Issues like the death of Michael Collins in 1922 are still reverberating around the area. Going back over the *Cork Examiner* for over 150 years is the history of the area in microcosm and indeed in great detail."

Ted Crosbie, chairman of Cork Examiner Publications.

Walter McGrath, editor of the Cork *Holly Bough*.

Jack Lynch, a former Taoiseach, recalls his childhood memories of the *Evening Echo*, Cork's evening newspaper.

The *Cork Examiner* is a place of family dynasties among many members of staff, including printers and journalists. Five generations of Crosbies have owned and run the paper for the past 121 years, bringing it through turbulent times past and present. Yet the first Crosbie on the paper, Thomas, nearly did not take over the *Cork Examiner*. He had been offered a job as a leader writer on the London *Times* for the princely sum of 700 guineas a year, now worth around £50,000. The offer was withdrawn when they discovered that he was a Catholic. Ted Crosbie describes how many of the family work on the paper nowadays.

"Five, no six actually, there are the two senior directors, George Crosbie and myself, and then there are three other Crosbie directors, Alan, Billy and Tom, and then there is another Crosbie working as an artist in the place."

Tim Cramer talks about what it is like working on the *Cork Examiner*. "Well, there has always been a family atmosphere in the *Examiner*. It's been very much a family job over the generations, and in fact I think at the moment you will probably find some people whose grandparents and great-grandparents were employed here. It's good in some ways; I think it gives continuity and you know the sort of people they are. You know their strengths and weaknesses. They tend to have a fierce pride in the place and in the job and they tend to carry on accordingly."

But times move on. Margaret Jennings achieved a notable first when she joined the paper.

"I became the first female sub-editor with the *Examiner*. Of course, my background in running a Roscommon paper, which involved sub-editing and editing, stood by me to break new ground in this respect. But in moving into the *Examiner* I had to adapt to the new technology which was very exciting and which is changing all aspects of the business. The *Examiner* has been to the forefront of the newspaper business in Ireland in the new technology field. In May 1976 it became the first daily paper in Ireland to make the change, and plans are afoot at the moment to even develop this further, which will affect the organisation in a major way.

"It wasn't that difficult to work with so many men because my colleagues are very supportive and my Roscommon experience helped, where I had to deal over the stone with hot metal with the printers, the old-style printing people, so in coming into the *Examiner* I found the transition very easy. The printers and my fellow sub-editors here were extremely supportive. It's fun as well being a female amongst men. Blessed am I amongst men!"

She continued about the opportunities coming from employment equality. "I think that a male viewpoint of what would be generally recognised as a traditionally female situation can be very fresh. In the same way, I think a female viewpoint of generally traditional male situations, like the changing room in sport, can bring a fresh approach."

Newspapers always change. Heartbreak and humour go hand-in-hand and Tim Cramer remembers one amusing incident. "One particular story I do recall - there are so many of them - about a chap who was the sort of general factotum in the printing office: Nelius O'Callaghan, who was an elderly man at that stage and would have been contemporaneous with the then chairman Thomas Crosbie, who was the father of Ted Crosbie, our present chairman. Old Tom Crosbie took the occasional ramble into the printing floor at night just to feel how things were going and he and Nelius O'Callaghan were quite good pals. One night he came in, and he was passing by and he said, 'Good evening, Nelius.' The later replied, 'Good evening, Mr Crosbie', and then just as Tom Crosbie was walking away he called him back and he said, 'Excuse me, Mr Crosbie, could you tell me something please.' 'Of course', said Tom, 'I will if I can. What is it?' 'Could you tell me, sir, am I satisfactory?' Thomas Crosbie was taken very aback and he said, 'For heaven's sake, Nelius, what's wrong with you, why are you asking that question?' 'Well, it's like this, sir. When I came in fifty years ago I was told that if I was satisfactory I would be kept on, but nobody ever came back to tell me if I was satisfactory. Could you please tell me if I am satisfactory?' The whole office just disintegrated into laughter."

Nostalgia, too, plays its part. For many years the *Holly Bough* has been a familiar part of Christmas in Cork as Walter McGrath, a retired employee and long-time editor of the publication, recounts.

"The *Holly Bough* was originally the Christmas organ of the *Cork Weekly Examiner*, a famous part of the firm. It sent out up to 50,000 copies every week to home and abroad; it was especially the exiles' paper and they all looked forward to receiving the weekly from their relatives back at home. The paper contained a lot of local news of interest to people living away from home. Then once a year it produced this colourful magazine. In the early days, it had a red holly or a red berry cover and that was why it was called the *Holly Bough* and in more recent years it is in full colour."

The Cork *Holly Bough* is still going strong. But the old *Cork Weekly Examiner* came to an end twelve years ago, in 1981. "I suppose it was the last of the weeklies published by what was primarily a daily firm and it certainly did not go without many regrets and there were protests from the people in England and America, but I would have liked to see it continue. There are still people who pine for it, but I suppose the times were against it."

Jack Lynch still remembers with affection one of his favourite columnists in the old *Weekly Examiner*. "He was Paddy Mehigan. His sons are well known in Dublin in medical circles. He wrote the wonderful 'Carbery's Column', mainly about Gaelic games and racy of the soil and of course he used his great idiomatic West Cork language and repertoire; he was a great writer. He was the first, I think, Gaelic sports commentator on RTE and he was succeeded by the great Michael O'Hehir."

The *Cork Examiner* under its present editor, Fergus O'Callaghan, sees itself as an alternative national newspaper voice coming from outside Dublin. In the capital itself there is a steady demand for the Cork accent on the nation's affairs as Ted Crosbie makes clear.

"Well, Dublin itself has a good tight circulation of about 2,000 copies a day. Some of them would be Cork people living in Dublin, some of them would be civil servants and more of them would be members of the general public who like to see the alternative voice coming from not necessarily the Dublin area. But as for fun, there is always fun in a newspaper office. Some of it you wouldn't say over what should be a family radio programme."

Chapter 13

The Derry Papers

• • •

DERRY CITY ENCAPSULATES MUCH of the newspaper history of Northern Ireland, indeed, the whole of Ireland, since its two main local titles, the *Derry Journal* and the *Londonderry Sentinel* are among the oldest papers in Ireland. The pedigree of the *Belfast Telegraph*, which has published in Derry for almost all of this century, stretches back to 1870. The *Derry Journal* is the third oldest paper in Ireland, established in 1772; only the *Newsletter* in Belfast (1737) and the *Limerick Chronicle* (1766) can claim longer antecedents.

In another way, too, the Derry papers encapsulate social history in the North of Ireland. The *Derry Journal* is read mainly by the nationalist community, while the *Sentinel* is the organ of the unionist community in and around the city, and the Derry edition of the *Belfast Telegraph* stands somewhere in the middle ground.

Yet the *Derry Journal* started off as a conservative paper for the Protestant community, and it was only when it changed its politics early in the nineteenth century that the *Sentinel* came into being. The very first issue of the *Derry Journal* was published on Wednesday, 3 June 1772; its full title was the *London-Derry Journal and General Advertiser*. Its founder was George Douglas, and it was printed at a stationery shop in the Diamond belonging to James Blyth, of whom Douglas was presumably a tenant. This very first issue, consisting of four pages, was the city's first newspaper.

The first issue did not make a promising start commercially, since all the advertisements fitted into a single column, but for the past 221 years the paper has appeared without significant breaks in publication. However, publication arrangements have varied considerably; sometimes, the paper was a weekly, at other times, a tri-weekly, and for a brief period

Paper Tigers

Masthead from the *Derry Journal*.

A portent of the future: in the early 1950s, the RUC prevented nationalists in Derry from marching. On the extreme left of the photograph is Frank McCarroll, then owner of the *Derry Journal*. The big man at the front of the group is Eddie McAteer, leader of the old Nationalist Party.

in 1877, a daily. In October 1772, just four months after the paper was launched, publication was changed to Tuesdays and Fridays. In 1958, after over eighty years of publication three times a week, it reverted to the format introduced in October 1772, Tuesdays and Fridays, and has remained so ever since.

An early indication of the founding politics of the paper can be gained from an advertisement run in the paper by George Douglas, who sought an apprentice to the printing trade. The person required had to be a "Protestant and well recommended".

A sea change overcame the Derry newspaper business in 1829. The *Derry Journal* had been doing very well as a Protestant paper, despite the general slump in trade during the early part of the nineteenth century. In 1815 its printing works and offices were tranferred the short distance from the Diamond to Shipquay Street; the direct and indirect employment the paper gave was considerable. Even the newsprint used was produced locally, probably at McClintock's paper mill near Clady in County Derry.

During the year 1829, one of the landmark years of modern Irish history, Catholic Emancipation was introduced in law and the *London-Derry Journal* gave up any pretensions of being a conservative newspaper; in a radical change of editorial policy, it decided to support Emancipation. For over half a century, the paper had been the only newspaper in the north-west, covering Derry and Donegal especially, but the editor of the *Derry Journal*, William Wallen, resigned to set up a new paper which would continue the conservative tradition.

The new *Londonderry Sentinel* attracted many subscribers from all over the north-west and was an immediate success. Yet the *Derry Journal* continued to prosper; by 1837 Edward Hyslop had become the owner and set about installing new typesetting and printing equipment. For the first six months of that year, he claimed that the circulation of the *Derry Journal* had gone up by 312 copies a week over the same period of 1836, a substantial increase for a time when heavy stamp duty was imposed on newspapers.

Over at the *Sentinel*, whose own history was somewhat sketchily covered in its 150th anniversary supplement in 1979, Wallen died. A James Colhoun, who had been associated with the paper from the very start, took over, in conjunction with Wallen's widow, then went into partnership with Thomas Chambers, a solicitor and a former under-sheriff for Derry City and County. After twenty years' partnership between Colhoun and Chambers, Colhoun became the sole owner.

The *Sentinel* remained in the ownership of the Colhoun family for a century. James Colhoun was succeeded as sole owner by his son William, who died in 1915. William's son James then took over; like his father, he was a president of the City and Foyle Unionist Association, a strong indication of the paper's intimate links with the city establishment, then profoundly unionist. James served in the Royal Inniskilling Fusiliers in the First World War and subsequently always used his title of major. He was also awarded the Military Cross during the Great War. The two sons of Major James Colhoun died tragically young, both from illness rather than accident. Samuel died in 1939, aged nineteen, while William died in 1943, aged twenty. James himself died on 6 September 1945. His widow, Florence, and her brother, William Rodden, a Belfast accountant, took over the paper, and so it continued until 1958 when it was bought by John Morton of Lurgan, his son James and son-in-law G. Courtney Hutchinson. After their takeover, they changed the paper to tabloid size, similar to its original size back in 1829.

Through the nineteenth century, other papers came and went in the city, including the *Londonderry Chronicle* (1829-72), the *Londonderry Guardian* (1857-71) and the *Londonderry Reporter* (1810-11). Other titles which proved ephemeral included the *Londonderry Recorder* and the *North West Farmer*. But the *Londonderry Standard*, established in 1836, proved rather more enduring, lasting for 128 years.

In the *Londonderry Sentinel* of 10 September 1836, a prospectus for a new paper, the *Londonderry Standard*, appeared. "The landed and trading interests of the country shall occupy a considerable portion of the columns of the *Standard*", it said, "and the paper would be the Guardian and Defender of those precious Civil and Religious Institutions for which our forefathers fought and conquered." The *Standard*, it was promised, would be printed with a new and beautiful type and on a paper of superior quality and would be the only paper published twice weekly in the north-west.

However, the first issue did not appear on the second Wednesday of October that year as promised, due to delays by the type founders, and did not emerge, in fact, until 30 November. In that year, the electorate of the city amounted to just over 500 people, out of a population of nearly 17,000. In 1870 the paper, then well established, had a chance of demonstrating its liberal credentials by supporting the Land Act, which gave farmers fixity of tenure, a fair rent and the liberty of free sale.

For many decades, through war and peace, prosperity and economic decline, the *Standard* soldiered on, the third of Derry's papers, printed and published in Shipquay Street in close proximity to the then offices of the *Derry Journal*, which had changed its name from the *Londonderry Journal* in 1880. The *Sentinel*, now in Strand Road, was then in Pump Street.

The early years of this century saw another addition to Derry's newspaper ranks, the *Derry People and Donegal News*, part of the *Ulster Herald* group. This paper has its main office in Omagh and an office also in Letterkenny, where the *Derry Journal* also has its Donegal office. The inaugural issue of the *Derry People and Donegal News* appeared on 20 September 1902, priced one penny. Printed by the *Ulster Herald*, it was published at Richmond Street, Derry. In its first issue, it declared that it was a "national journal, and will support the movement to make our native land a real Irish Ireland". From the first issue, one of its most prominent features was its "Irish Ireland" column, which had notes and comments on the Irish Revival movement, especially in the north-west.

A broadsheet, the new paper got off to a good start, with eight pages in its first issue and plenty of advertising. In line with newspaper custom of that time, the front page was made up entirely of small advertisements. By the end of that year, the *Derry People and Donegal News* was making obvious progress. Its Christmas issue, published on 20 December 1902, contained a special supplement for the festival and ran to all of sixteen pages.

Two years later, its political antithesis appeared, the *Irish Daily Telegraph*, as High Tory as its London namesake. Fred Potter, the renowned editor of the unionist-inclined *Skibbereen Eagle* in West Cork, had published a paper of this same name in Cork City between 1871 and 1873. This *Irish Daily Telegraph*, however, was published by the Bairds, owners of the *Belfast Telegraph*. Printed in Belfast, it was launched in 1904, published in both Derry and Newry and containing a predominance of cross-channel news but with reasonable local news coverage.

Derry's next newspaper upheaval came in early 1932, when J. C. Glendinning, who had owned and edited the *Standard* for many years, proposed to retire. He consulted with his managers. R. M. Thompson had come to the paper many years previously from Manchester and ran the printing, bookbinding and paper ruling departments, while Thomas Joyce was the manager of the newspaper and publishing departments of the paper, then published three times weekly. D. P. Thompson, the company secretary, had joined the paper in his native city back in 1893 and was a staunch trade unionist, which gave an inkling of the developments to come.

The workers on the paper then decided to acquire the paper themselves and run it as a co-operative, otherwise they could well have been left without a job on the owner's retirement. A total of twenty-four shareholders each took a share of one hundred pounds in the new company, a considerable sum in those days. The new company became owners of the *Derry Standard* on 1 July 1932. The chief reporter, Thomas Parke, was appointed editor; he had come from Strabane in 1914 to work on the paper. It was said of him in the 1936 centenary supplement of the *Derry Standard* that "his leading articles are read with much admiration and interest throughout the United Kingdom". Despite the best intentions of the new owners and the workers, the paper lasted for just another twenty-eight years.

The year that the *Derry Standard* was taken over by its workers, 1932, saw one of the century's great Irish newspaper scoops. Cecil A. King, then chief reporter of the *Derry Journal*, who later went on to run the *Donegal Democrat* in Ballyshannon, heard a plane going over while he was reading, over lunch, about the American woman flyer, Amelia Earhart, heading for Ireland. He jumped into a taxi and headed out of Derry on the Culmore Road, towards Moville, and when he walked into a field met up with the flyer, who gave him an exclusive interview. Among the other Derry reporters who covered the story was Cecil Milligan, who that year had been promoted from chief reporter to editor of the *Sentinel*, following the retirement of J. C. Orr.

While the *Derry Journal* had that great scoop in 1932, in 1946 the *Sentinel* scooped the world by announcing that the Soviet Union had followed the lead of the US by developing the atomic bomb. During the Second World War, Derry port had been busy with Royal Navy and US Navy ships and this more cosmopolitan atmosphere brought interesting characters to the city. Sidney Buchanan, then and for many years after the editor of the *Sentinel*, interviewed a West African scientist working in Derry during the war, a Dr Armattoe, about the USSR bomb. The story produced immediate official denials, but the calls flooded in to Sidney Buchanan from the international news agencies. Three weeks later, the USSR admitted its work in nuclear weapons' development: Buchanan's scoop had been totally accurate.

After the war was over, the overseas service people left, and Derry reverted to its then normal state, a forbidding city in which its nationalist citizens, a majority of the population, had second-class rights. Yet even in those grim times, humour and fun broke through. On one royal visit to the city, in the immediate post-war period, the royal party had been due to travel from Belfast by train, but for security reasons went by road instead. However, the journalists covering the visit still went by train, and so splendid was the hospitality that by the time they arrived in Derry, the press corps was a well-oiled machine.

Terry Ward of the *Irish Press*, where calling the Six Counties "Northern Ireland" was almost a sacking offence in those far-off days, was a Derryman with impeccable republican credentials; he had begun his newspaper career on the *Derry Journal*. When he got off the train at Waterside station to cover that royal visit, his knowing colleagues were amused to see him walking the red carpet to be greeted officially by an RUC inspector.

When Ben Kiely from Omagh was the literary editor of the *Irish Press*, Jim McGuinness, editor of that paper for much of the 1950s and himself another Derryman, gave him another royal marking in Derry. "Get out of your corner and go up and meet the Queen" were his instructions. So Ben got himself up to Derry and met up with Mick Cannon, then a noted Belfast-based newspaper correspondent. Before he had even left Dublin, Ben had written the headline for his piece: "No flags on the Lecky Road", referring to what he described as the nationalist backbone of Derry.

The night before the visit, Ben Kiely and Mick Cannon met up with Brian Friel, the playwright, himself an Omagh man, and his father - a lovely man in Ben Kiely's estimation - in a pub on the Lecky Road. Ben said to an old man in the pub that the Queen wasn't going to have much time in Derry. The old man turned around and remarked: "She won't have time to piss in Derry." Later, Ben found that this was untrue: "I discovered they had a special place fixed up in the Guildhall for the Queen to sit on if she felt like it." Ben remembers that various Derrywomen including "a great singing lady in Derry, Josephine O'Doherty" sat on the same seat so that they could say that they had sat where the Queen had.

During the next morning, Mick Cannon and Ben Kiely went to the royal garden party in Brooke Park. "In the middle of the ceremony, we felt like going to the gentlemen's. There was no question of wild security or anything like that at the time. We came out, having just buttoned ourselves up, and we walked between a procession of parked cars, bang in front of the Queen and Prince Philip. The party was over and they were going to get into their car."

In the distance, remembers Ben Kiely, was George Leitch, "a wee crusty man with a moustache", well known for years as the principal photographer with *The Irish Times*. He was waving his camera, shouting, "Hold it, hold it". Later, Ben asked him what he was supposed to say to the Queen that would have stopped her in her tracks. Leitch replied: "You could have said that a member of the Royal Flying Corps [the First World War predecessor of the RAF] was rushing up to take a picture." Ben Kiely says that to this day, he regrets that he hadn't thought of that, so that there would have been a remarkable picture of de Valera's two men with the Queen and Prince Philip.

By 1952, one of Derry's papers had run its course, the *Irish Daily Telegraph*. It remained the traditional broadsheet format and in its page layout and content remained close to the *Daily Telegraph* in London, and not dissimilar either in its political viewpoint. On the front page, it had a late news box, with news printed in blue. Late news and special late editions of papers produced for great events have been ousted by radio and television. The assassination of President Kennedy in November 1963 was one of the last occasions that any Irish newspaper turned out a special late edition.

But in late April 1952 a small notice appeared on the front of the *Irish Daily Telegraph*: "The proprietors intimate that on and after Thursday next [1 May], the *Irish Daily Telegraph* will be merged in the *Belfast Telegraph* and will be replaced by the latter title." Readers were promised the Late Final Edition, with a more comprehensive service of general and sports news. From that point, the *Belfast Telegraph* built up its Derry edition, changing a limited number of pages from the Belfast editions. But the paper's Derry edition has always been overshadowed by its Belfast big brother; when the *Belfast Telegraph* published its centenary supplement in September 1970, it contained not a word about its Derry editorial, advertising and printing operations over the years.

Four years after the closure of the *Irish Daily Telegraph* in 1952 came the closure of the *Derry Weekly News*, which had been published for sixty years. A much greater shock came in 1964 when the *Derry Standard* closed, although like the passing of a frail, elderly relative, the news was not unexpected in the city. Many of the people on the paper who had been involved in its co-operative takeover in 1932 had then been heading towards middle age. Now they were old men, with no obvious successors, so the *Standard*, for so long a proud tradition in Derry newspaper publishing, expired. Under Morton control, its main pro-unionist competitor, the *Sentinel*, had become much more commercially aggressive.

Time moved on, but more positively with the other Derry papers. The *Derry Journal* has had remarkably few editors this century. Paddy Flanagan, a native of Buncrana, County Donegal, was editor through the war years into the 1950s. When he retired in 1957, he was succeeded by Tom Cassidy. The first few years of his occupancy of the editor's chair saw the usual daily and weekly torments of any newspaper editor. But in the early 1960s, the first signs of the dissent long bubbling beneath the surface in Derry came to light. Concern about gerrymandering in the city, and general dismay about the Stormont government's decision to put the new University of Ulster in Coleraine rather than Derry, helped ignite the first sparks, first of the civil rights movement, then of more serious troubles.

Derry's famous civil rights march of October 1968, which drew a certain inspiration from the student movement's paralysing actions in Paris in May that year, drew world-wide attention to a long-festering situation. In August 1969, the first British troops arrived in the North, in Derry, and the present Troubles (not the first in the North by any means) were under way.

For Tom Cassidy, it was a baptism of fire, literally. Almost overnight, he was propelled from being editor of one of Ireland's oldest and leading regional newspapers to having one of the toughest jobs in European journalism. Bloody Sunday at the end of January 1972 was perhaps the most difficult time of all. Thirteen Derry people were killed on the streets of their city, and another died some time later. The local paper, the *Derry Journal*, was the only channel open to many Derry people to vent their anger and their anguish. According to many of his colleagues of the time, the pressures on Tom Cassidy were "simply unbelievable". Pat McArt, the present editor, says that there is little doubt the stress affected Tom's health, although he did not retire until 1977.

Even though the Troubles were coming to the first of their many crescendi, the *Derry Journal* was still moving ahead. By the end of the 1960s, its Cossar press was outliving its useful life, taking at least ten hours to print the paper. On 6 February 1970, the first web offset printed issue of the paper appeared. At first, the company's new premises on the Buncrana Road were used for platemaking and printing, but by February 1971, all departments had moved there and the old premises in Shipquay Street were sold to the Derry Development Commission. In 1974 the *Belfast Telegraph* updated its Derry arrangements, moving into new purpose-built premises in the city, where it could produce up to four separate pages of news and advertisements for its Derry and north-west editions.

When Tom Cassidy retired, a legendary figure in north-west journalism became editor, Frank Curran, who had a rare mix of interests, sport and politics. Nearly ten years ago, he produced a very popular local book, *The History of Derry City FC Club*, a work that was a labour of love. During forty years of soccer reporting for the *Derry Journal*, he only missed a few games.

But Frank Curran is even more interested in politics. As far back as 1945, when no one in the Northern establishment wanted to listen, he wrote a book entitled *Ireland's Fascist City*, about the gerrymandering in Derry City, which left its two-thirds nationalist population being governed by representatives of the minority unionist population. In 1984 he published *Derry - A Countdown to Disaster*, described as the definitive history of what led to the outbreak of the Troubles in Derry in 1968. When Frank Curran stepped down from the editorial chair on 1 February 1982, he had completed forty years' unbroken service with the *Derry Journal*. Also in 1982, William O'Connell, a compositor with the *Derry Journal*, was elected mayor of the city.

Frank Curran's successor is the present editor, Pat McArt, a native of Letterkenny, County Donegal, and the youngest editor in the paper's history. Appointed editor at the age of twenty-eight, he had been a member of the political unit in RTE, having begun his career in Letterkenny with the *Derry People and Donegal News*.

Today the *Derry Journal* is going better than ever, published on Tuesdays and Fridays. The Tuesday edition sells about 24,000 copies, while that on Fridays sells about 26,500. In addition, the company produces a freesheet on Wednesdays, the *Journal Extra*, which is delivered to 28,000 homes in the Derry City area.

The *Sentinel*, too, is still going strong, although it sells about a quarter as many copies as the *Derry Journal*. Still, the newspaper tradition in Derry is thriving, more than 200 years after it began, a remarkable contribution to the history of newspaper publishing in Ireland.

Chapter 14

The Meath and Louth Papers

• • •

NEWSPAPERS IN COUNTIES MEATH and Louth draw from deep journalistic wells. But times change, and Margot Davis, editor and publisher of *Modern Woman*, Ireland's only paper for women, produced in Navan, details one recent readership survey.

"I suppose the most controversial one has been the sex survey. We did that about two years ago; we didn't know how women were going to react to it. It was something new to us and indeed new to this country because it had never been done before, a very open sex survey. Actually they reacted to it very well, the opposite to how I thought they would. They wrote in with their views and how they felt about sex, which I think is a very natural thing. We waited for the replies and they started pouring in; it actually amazed us. Our youngest was sixteen and a half and the oldest was sixty-five."

Margot Davis's husband, Jack, who is managing director of the *Meath Chronicle*, explains where the paper began. "The old *Chronicle* was in fact started in Kells by the Daly family in 1897 and it had a chequered history in its founding years. My grandfather James Davis took over its printing. He printed it in Navan in the old printing works, under contract for the Daly family. About 1912 he bought the publishing rights of the paper and it has been in our family since that particular time. There have been various editors down since that time. Our present editor is my co-director James Davis."

A new generation, equally enthusiastic, is coming up in the paper: James's son Ken and Jack's children Paul and Edward. Navan also has a much newer paper, the tabloid *Weekender*, a bright and breezy weekly founded ten years ago. In total contrast, the Dundalk *Democrat* is one of

The caseroom in the *Meath Chronicle* about 1916, with cases of hand-held type and hand-operated printing equipment.

A newspaper printing press at the *Meath Chronicle* in 1914: it printed two pages on one side of the sheet and was in use until the late 1950s.

Paul Murphy, present editor of the *Drogheda Independent*.

the oldest weekly newspapers in the country, dating back nearly 150 years. Very unusually among weekly newspapers, the *Democrat* still keeps to the real old style for its front page, no news at all, just advertisements. The *Drogheda Independent* began in 1884 with the help of Parnell, Davitt and an Augustinian priest, Father Anderson. Michael Casey became editor in 1887 and remained rooted to the editor's chair for an incredible fifty-two years. One of his sons, Peter, editor from 1940, had a total of fifty-six years in journalism with the paper. Paul Murphy is the present editor.

"I started my journalistic career in Drogheda with the *Drogheda Independent* and some years later - 1966 - I joined Independent Newspapers and have been working for the group since then. I moved to Drogheda in 1985. It's nice to be editor of the paper in your home town. The paper was taken over by Independent Newspapers in the late 1960s, and then later still, in 1973, the group was taken over by present chairman Tony O'Reilly."

Drogheda in particular has a long tradition of newspaper competition, most recently the now defunct *Local News*. Paul Murphy talks about the 1978 start-up of the *Drogheda Express*. "It was a tabloid newspaper, bright and breezy, but there were two papers pulling out of the same pool of advertising. While it was a journalistic success, many people thought it wasn't an advertising or commercial success."

But the expansionary theme has continued. In Navan the *Meath Chronicle*, with a very solid circulation, also produces its *Provincial Farmer* supplement and prints about thirty other publications. Margot Davis describes the origins of *Modern Woman*.

"I started it thirteen years ago, with a colour supplement in the *Meath Chronicle,* and it became very popular. The women loved it. Then four years ago we decided we would go nationwide; I have never looked back. But I was very nervous in the beginning, mind you. I can remember the first day when it went out on the streets; I remember going into the newsagents and looking at all the glossy magazines and there was *Modern Woman* with all the newspapers and I thought, 'Oh my God, am I going to sell one or am I going to sell any at all?' I was very nervous. It was completely new to me. But it really took off from there and we never looked back. When I started off four years ago nationwide, I wanted something that was going to improve, I wanted something that would give women something to look forward to every month, so that they would say, 'This is the time it is coming out and we have to get it.' And every month it comes off the press, my first impulse is to look through the paper, find the faults and improve on them. I have done that from the word go. I want to aim at giving women something that is their own, something they can actually look up to and say, 'Look, this is our paper', and so far that's the reaction I am getting from them too.

"I found it very difficult in the beginning, coping with the Dublin media, I must say. I found that when you come in from a country town, even though you have a national paper, they still think of you as being country. And when you come from ten miles out of Dublin at all, you are a culchie. So they looked on me as a culchie. I was going up there with a paper on my own and I found the reaction was, 'Oh well, look, she's a nobody. You know, she really isn't very important, she just comes from Navan.' But now I find that after four years of struggling, they are beginning to accept me and say, 'Well, look, she's not too bad after all. Look what she is doing.'"

Paul Murphy of the *Drogheda Independent* explains how that group of newspapers has spread its interests with the *Fingal Independent*. "That's a new development for the newspaper. We did have a certain circulation in north County Dublin and we tried to expand the role of the paper in that area, stretching from the airport to just north of Balbriggan, an area which has a rapidly growing population and its own Fingal Council. We find there is a whole new readership out there and we have gone after it and very successfully so."

For the *Mid-Louth Independent*, three pages are changed from the *Drogheda Independent*, while in Dundalk a sister paper, the *Argus*, is gaining ground. "It has its own editor, Kevin Mulligan, it has its own journalistic and advertising staff in Dundalk and is a very successful newspaper with a rapidly growing circulation. Sales have gone up from about 4,000 to over 8,000 a week and it is regarded as one of the success stories within the *Independent* group."

Paul Murphy talks about the rival Dundalk paper. "The Dundalk *Democrat* still has all advertisements on the front page and it doesn't carry news stories there. It's a traditional newspaper and it has its own circulation in Dundalk. Whereas the Dundalk *Democrat* might be regarded as a paper of record, the *Argus* is very much a story-driven newspaper."

But change was not always welcomed. George Smith, the circulation manager of the *Meath Chronicle*, remembers when the paper was one of the first weeklies in Ireland to introduce numerous photographs on a regular basis, around thirty years ago.

"Some of the older people didn't like it, but some of the modern generation thought it was great. The development boosted up sales. We were one of the first provincials to have photographs and I must say the old klischograph did a very good job of them at that time; it was slow, but it was very good. The quality of pictures turned out was excellent. If the photographer used good-quality paper in his printing they came out very well."

The region has produced an amazing variety of journalistic talent over the years. People who started on the *Meath Chronicle* included Leo Enright, the broadcaster, and Jack Fagan, *Irish Times* property editor. Drogheda names have included Michael Hand, once an editor of the *Sunday Independent,* and George A. O'Gorman, who was editor of the *Drogheda Independent* before Paul Murphy. When Dave Allen, the comedian, was a youngster, he worked on the old *Argus* when it was based in Drogheda, wrapping up bundles of newspapers, filling in forms for small ads for births, marriages and deaths. Always the humour comes through. Anne Kane, sister of Drogheda journalist the late Tony Mathews who worked in the *Evening Press* and the RTE newsroom, has been a journalist herself on the *Drogheda Independent* for forty years and remembers one notorious scrape.

"One of our own reporters here, George Hussey, lost his job here as a young man. At that time the reporters used to have to proofread their copy and he was supposed to proofread a story about the funeral of a fairly important Protestant bishop. Instead of saying that the internment had taken place, he said the entertainment had taken place. His editor didn't care for that too much, and poor old George was sacked and he went off, spending some time in Africa. One of his proudest boasts used to be that he had shot black lion on the banks of the Limpopo River; he always had this great claim to fame afterwards. But he came back and settled down again. His job was given back to him and he worked here for thirty years as a reporter."

George Smith recalls one printing job at the *Meath Chronicle* which didn't quite work out as intended. "We were setting a poster one day and it was something like 'Thirty acres for sale'. Some guy switched it, so it read 'Thirty arses for sale'. It was never spotted, especially when there

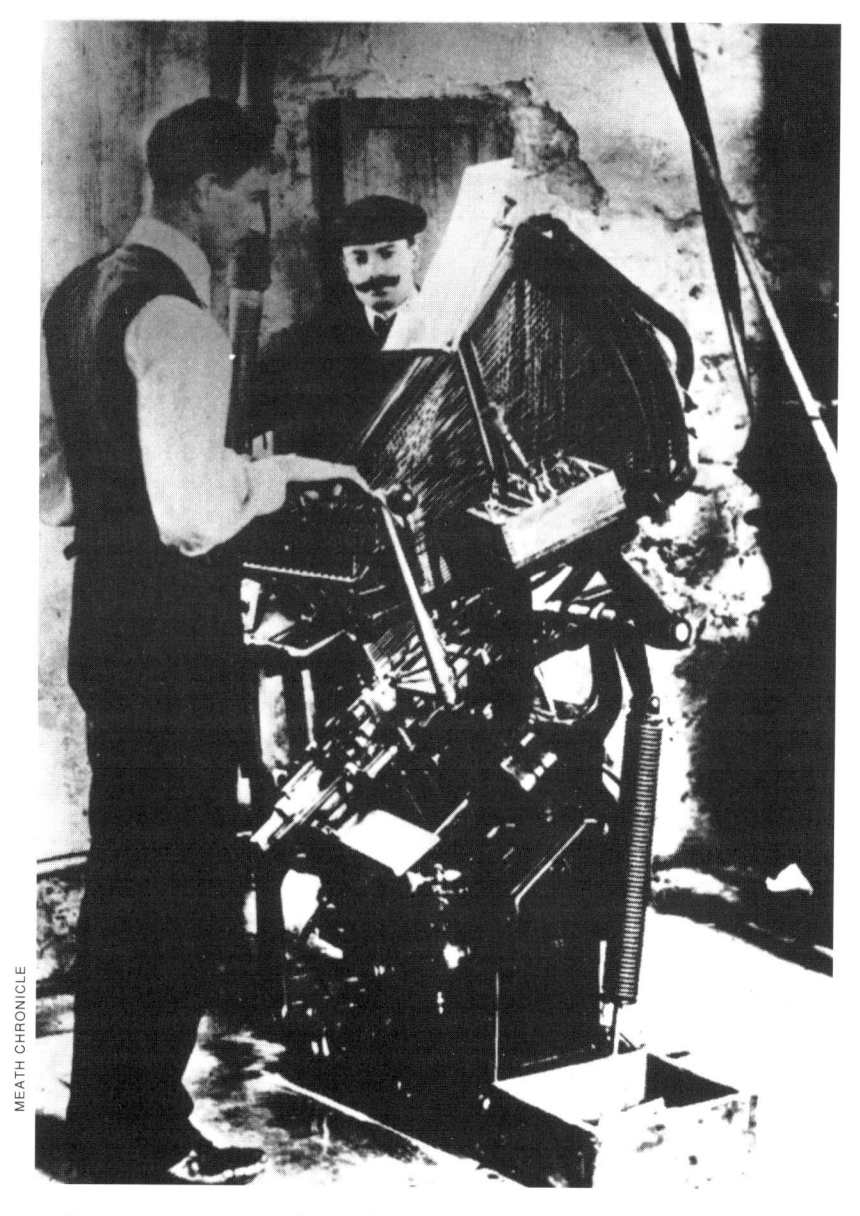

Matty McGoona, a great friend of Francis Ledwidge, the poet, working the first line-casting machine in the *Meath Chronicle* in 1912.

would be quite large type, that's when you would make a mistake, not the small type. Old man Davis nearly went spare. It was deliberately switched, so it was, deliberately switched. And it went out. That would be highly embarrassing."

Apart from all the funny stories, there was always a strong interest in poetry and traditional music, as George Smith brings to mind. "Gerry Caffrey was a great fiddle player. He used to do a lot of fiddling; people were very attracted to the old traditional music at that time. They used to go from house to house, playing the old traditional music. Some of the compositors here used to write poetry while they would be operating the Linotype. Marvellous, very intelligent individuals, but they used to maintain that all printers were a bit eccentric and it was blamed on the ink."

Francis Ledwidge from Slane was the most famous poet from the whole area. He wrote for the *Drogheda Independent*, had a brother working in the *Meath Chronicle* and was very friendly with a printer in the Navan paper called Mattie McGoona. Jack Davis remembers an amazing ghost story about Ledwidge coming back to the *Meath Chronicle* works during the First World War.

"There is an old story about Francis Ledwidge, he and Mattie McGoona were friends from childhood and they used to play pitch and toss. Ledwidge went off to the war anyway, and we heard nothing further until one day McGoona was working late in the *Meath Chronicle*. He came out of the old archway there, at about 2.00 in the morning, and lo and behold who did he walk into, only Francis, waiting outside. 'It's great to see you', says Francis, 'and I am delighted to see you still going. Of course, I lost my sweetheart', he says. 'Unfortunately, there is going to be bad news for you, you are going to get bad news about me in a few days' time', he said. They exchanged pleasantries and off they went. 'I didn't know Francis was back from the war', said Mattie McGoona, who puzzled over this meeting.

"About a week or so afterwards he heard that Francis Ledwidge had been killed at the front and he made further enquiries and lo and behold, he discovered that the very night that he was talking to him was the night Francis Ledwidge was actually killed. He puzzled over that and said, 'Well, of course we were great friends and what can one friend do but only come back to the other and say goodbye.'"

Chapter 15

The Evening Press

∴

WHEN THE *EVENING PRESS* was launched in Dublin in September 1954, it was a revolutionary moment, not only for the conservative *Irish Press* group, but for newspaper publishing in Ireland. Douglas Gageby, later a long-serving editor of *The Irish Times*, was its first editor.

"There is a picture of Betty Whelan on the top of page one in the first edition showing a bit of cleavage; nobody would notice it, of course, now. In the second edition it was deemed wise to do a little air brushing", he remembers.

He goes on to describe how there were two papers doing very well in the group, the *Irish Press* founded by Eamon de Valera and his friends in 1931 and then the *Sunday Press* which had been founded in 1949 when Sean Lemass was managing director. "In 1954 Vivion de Valera was managing director and he thought he should round off things by having a third paper. The obvious reasons were for revenue, for mopping up more advertising, but the secondary reason was to look for a different readership, an urban readership. While the *Sunday Press* had a certain proportion, it was rather lacking in the *Irish Press*. So Vivion and Jack Dempsey, who was then general manager, saw this paper as being something that would reach out to a new audience. They particularly had in mind the fact, as Dempsey said to me often, 'half the people on this island are women and our papers are too political and too stuffed with sport. We want a newer paper, we want a paper that will interest women and not just cookery and things like that.'" Douglas Gageby says that was very far seeing in 1953, when they first approached him to know if he would be interested in editing this new paper.

The new paper attracted some of the brightest talent around, people

The Evening Press

Below: Con Houlihan, *Evening Press* sports columnist, who hand writes one paragraph of copy to each sheet of paper.

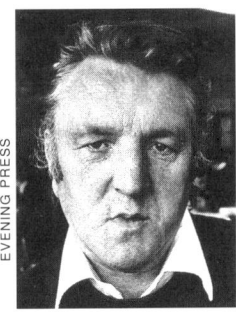

Above: Deirdre McSharry in 1955. She graduated from acting and modelling to journalism and worked on the *Evening Press* immediately after it was launched in 1954. Later, she won renown as long-time editor of *Cosmopolitan*, the UK-published women's magazine.

Noeleen Dowling, assistant features editor of the *Evening Press*.

Michael O'Toole, who wrote the nightly "Dubliner's Diary" in the *Evening Press* until early 1993.

like John Healy, Mick Finlan, Brian Cleeve, Deirdre McSharry, John O'Donovan and Terry O'Sullivan. Several of them came from the *Irish Press*; Jim McGuinness, then editor of the *Irish Press*, was very generous in letting some people move over, notably John O'Donovan, the chief sub-editor. The lynchpin in the news gathering was Jack Smyth, a Galwayman who had been a war correspondent for Reuters, whom Douglas Gageby had met in Berlin years before.

"We had the help of Dick Wilkes, a very big man in the *Irish Press* in those days. We had Terry O'Sullivan, of course, who had worked with me and others on the *Sunday Press*. We had a new young boy called Jim Downey, who is still going very well indeed. We had Tim Pat Coogan, later an editor of the *Irish Press* and still going very well. We had Des Moore who wrote historical pieces, still going well, Sean Cronin and Dan O'Connell. Mick Finlan is still going strong as the Galway correspondent of *The Irish Times*. John Healy was there, already bursting with news and information and he was a big figure too. Perhaps one of the best sellers we had was a feature called 'Wild Wisdom' by Ashton Freeman. I had always wanted to run a comic strip about nature and when I was appointed editor I went to Ashton Freeman who wrote about nature, while his wife illustrated. He said, 'Yea, great idea.' So we ran a daily adventure, 'Wild Wisdom' by Ashton Freeman and Stella Gore, all about the life of badgers and foxes and so on, running stories aimed at young children, really; it was fascinating stuff and did very well. Joe Sherwood was, I suppose, the best sports columnist of his time and we had among the brighter young sparks Deirdre McSharry, who had been doing acting and modelling and who later went on to become long-serving editor of the UK-published *Cosmopolitan* magazine."

The new paper had a real showbiz start, as Douglas Gageby recalls. "Oh, yes, we had an elephant. The *Irish Press* had just moved into Elephant House in O'Connell Street at the corner of Middle Abbey Street, and the late Dave Luke, a wonderful fellow, hired an elephant from the zoo to lead the procession up and down O'Connell Street. In fact, the paper didn't go well at the beginning. We had a bad time for the first few weeks. It always takes time for a paper to settle down and we really didn't get our first lift until the paper found the missing kidnapped Berrigan baby. The *Evening Press* discovered the baby and we had this story exclusively. We didn't run the machines at 2.00 pm for that edition. We didn't run the machines at 3.00 for the 3.00 pm edition, we didn't run them at 3.30 for the 3.30 pm edition, but at 3.45 pm we started roaring off, so that the other papers, the *Evening Herald* and the *Evening Mail,* couldn't pick it up in time. Dave Luke had a poster printed, so the exclusive was broadcast all over town."

The late John O'Donovan was one of the great journalistic characters of the paper, a dramatist, an expert on classical music and George Bernard Shaw, and a familiar broadcaster, known for years for his radio programme "Dear Sir or Madam".

"He was a vegetarian and a non-smoker and he used to be running up the windows and running them down in the *Evening Press* office. He was a very healthy fellow. They were all tremendous personalities. Terry O'Sullivan, of course, had a wonderful time. He used to come in about midnight or later with a couple of baby Powers whiskies and sit down in my office. I had an office - I sat all day in the open room, of course, but I had an office - and the caseroom overseer would drop in to see would it be late, would it be early, would it be long or what else, and they would have a little baby Powers and Terry would work away; then, in the early hours, they would have another baby Powers or two, it was quite a ritual. He was a remarkable figure, Terry, a lovely fellow; I had known him in the army. I knew him in various manifestations but he did his social column awfully well. He had a chauffeur-driven car because when he drove a car he tended to knock into lampposts. So he had a twenty-four-hour service, a wonderful thing in those days, 1954. I think he had a lot more cash than I had. He deserved it. Worked like hell", concludes Douglas Gageby.

In a radio interview, Terry O'Sullivan reminisced about his ways of working at Burgh Quay. "Every past couple of hours I bumped off, and bumped off is the word, about four or five harmless little glasses of wine. But the speed at which we had to work is because of the speed at which a newspaper is produced. The machines will not wait and no deadline will wait and that's all about it."

His successor who wrote "Dubliners Diary" in the *Evening Press* until early 1993 was Michael O'Toole. Since he joined the paper in 1964, he has seen many changes but remarkably few editors. He also expounds on the greatest danger in journalism - drink.

Interviewed in Mulligans in Poolbeg Street, a second "home" to generations of *Irish Press* journalists, he described how the pub is still very old fashioned. "You can't get a sandwich here and they don't serve coffee or any namby-pamby things like that." However, he explained that while in the old days drink had given rise to many humorous incidents in the newspaper business, the extent of present-day drinking by journalists had decreased enormously. "The Hollywood notion of hard-drinking journalists is very much dying out." In the old days, when Myles na gCopaleen (Flann O'Brien) wrote about the *Irish Press*, he remarked, somewhat humorously, that any piece of copy that went to the chief sub-editor without the imprimatur of a porter stain from a bottle of Guinness was automatically suspect.

Just as Michael O'Toole kept up the nightly and wearing diary tradition at the *Evening Press*, so Con Houlihan has succeeded Joe Sherwood as the big sportswriting personality. "Con and Joe have something in common as they are both controversialists, both splendid sports columnists. Joe did an enormous amount for the *Evening Press*, with his column called 'In the Soup'. But I much prefer Con's writing. He is a very serious man, but manages to write delightfully in a very light, readable way. He has ignored technological progress and writes his copy by hand on sheets of copy paper – cut-up newsprint or off-ends. He writes with a biro, one paragraph per page. He writes very spare paragraphs, almost like Hemingway, he loves the spare line. If one of his articles had, say, forty-two paragraphs, the manuscript would be made up of forty-two slips of paper. He has never used a typewriter to my knowledge; he writes at strange Cistercian hours of the morning, getting up, I think, about 4.00 am to write his column."

The *Evening Press* was the first paper in Ireland to make a conscious appeal to women readers. Traditionally, newspapers have always been male-dominated, created by men who nursed pints in Dublin's journalistic pubs, but at an early stage of the *Evening Press* women reporters and feature writers started coming to the fore. Noeleen Dowling, the assistant features editor, details their arrival.

"In the 1970s Clare Boylan, Nuala Fennell, Mary Kenny and a lot of other fine women news reporters began there. I think of Maureen Browne, now editor of the *Irish Medical Times*, Micheline McCormack who is assistant editor of the *Sunday World* and Muriel Reddy who is features editor of the *Age* newspaper in Melbourne, Australia. The real influx of women into the *Evening Press* was in the late 1960s and the level had been stepped up in the 1980s. So you had roughly half and half men and women news reporters, and of course fewer women in sports, fewer women in finance. That is changing now; there are more women employed in both sport and finance than there used to be. In features it wouldn't have changed very much, it would be about the same, about half and half. I would love to see a woman editor some day and I don't think there is any reason why we won't; there is certainly lots of talent there now on the way up. At assistant editor and sub-editor level there are women; they are pretty well represented. There is probably a need for more women in the sports area, but I think that is something that is coming."

But there is the down side, too. Both men and women have to cover the most harrowing stories. Noeleen Dowling's most horrific experience was the Stardust fire in 1981.

"It wasn't just the night of the disaster itself when, thank goodness, I wasn't working. But the following day we were all deployed around the city and I found myself over in the city morgue watching people identify personal belongings of people they had lost. That really was tremendously upsetting and difficult to cope with."

Journalists in the *Irish Press* group also have to work against a background of continual financial uncertainty. Michael O'Toole is famous for his humorous remark on the situation.

"I said it was akin to living over the San Andreas fault in California. But people get used to it. We've had difficult times here, including complex industrial relations problems, but it hasn't always been like that. I would hope and believe that we will come out of it and go back to that period between the 1960s and the 1980s, when it was a very, very happy ship indeed and we were leading the pack. I hope we get back to that again."

Chapter 16

The Mayo Papers

• • •

COUNTY MAYO, THAT LARGE WEST of Ireland county, full of striking land and seascapes, devastated by emigration, has had a unique reputation for producing national journalists in abundance. The best known, who started on the *Western People* in Ballina, was John Healy.

"He was a great journalist. He had an inimitable style of his own, very picturesque, and he was a good reporter. He had insight, he knew what was going on; if he didn't know, he could assess and he gave a great new dimension to political reporting. He was a great enthusiast, always bubbling with new ideas, suggestions, terribly interested in things like forestry, fishing and economic and social development of all kinds. My disagreement with him there would have been to try and hold him back, restrain him if that were possible, but he was so full of imagination and progressive thoughts and ideas. He was a stimulating person and at the end of the day I would have to say a very, very good Irishman."

That was former Taoiseach Charles J. Haughey paying tribute to his great friend, the County Mayo journalist John Healy who died nearly three years ago. Mayo is a county which has turned out probably more journalists for the national media than anywhere else in Ireland. Healy, from Charlestown, always liked to call himself simply reporter. Yet at one stage he took great pleasure in owning a white Rolls-Royce. Terry Reilly, the present managing editor of the *Western People*, printed and published in Ballina and largest of the three Mayo papers, remembers him starting off.

"John's first job was in newspapers. He lived in Charlestown which is about twenty-five miles from Ballina and he cycled down to an interview in Ballina with the editor at the time, the late Fred Devere, and John convinced him that he had the makings of a journalist. He worked for the princely sum of 2s. 6d. a week. I think he made an immediate impact; John was a tremendous journalist even at that stage and went on to edit the *Sunday Review* and do the 'Backbencher' column in *The Irish Times* and radio and TV work. He was a man who identified the moods of the time and the drift from the West even before other people did."

Ted Nealon, journalist turned politician, brings to mind the style of John Healy. "He was extraordinarily prolific, he was a powerful writer but he could get to the essence of a story. He could write with great ease, no problem at all, and then he had the other aspect of being a reporter, very important to his work, that whatever story he was doing, that was the most important story of the day."

Another journalist of renown who started on the *Western People* was Tom Hennigan, who went on to write the nightly diary column on the *Evening Herald*. Rita Devere Durcan, chairperson and majority shareholder of the *Western People*, has strong memories of him.

"Tom and I met in the early years of my involvement with the paper; he was effervescent. It was a pleasure to meet him; he was always in such wonderful humour and always ready for a joke of some kind or another. My late husband and he had a very strong relationship."

Before Tom Hennigan's time, J. F. Quinn was the doyen of Mayo journalists for many years. He wrote over 300 historical features for the *Western People*, now being republished in book form. Rita Devere Durcan summarises the spirit of the place: "The *Western People* was once described to me by the wife of a prominent politician as the cradle of genius."

The *Western People* itself had a most unusual birthplace, as Terry Reilly explains. "The Bishop invited the community to the Sacristy of St Muredach's Cathedral, Ballina, and they sat down, had their first meeting there and decided to open a subscription and get the paper up and going. It quickly established itself; looking back at the old issues, it jumped from six or eight pages right up to twenty pages in absolutely no time at all and commanded a wide readership."

Once County Mayo had four main papers, but the *Ballina Herald*, later incorporated into the *Western People*, closed down in 1962. In 1977 John Healy was a leading figure in the start up of the *Western Journal* which managed to last six years. Today, the county has three newspapers, the *Western People*, the *Connaught Telegraph* in Castlebar, and the *Mayo News* in Westport. The *Western People* may be nearly 110-years old, but the

T. H. Gillespie, the first member of the Gillespie family to own the
Connaught Telegraph; he died in 1939. This photograph was taken in the
early years of this century.

The late John Healy, the "backbencher" of *The Irish
Times*, who started his journalistic career with the
Western People in Ballina.

Billy Gallagher, long since retired, plating up the old Goss press which had been used in the *Western People* since the 1920s. In 1978 it was replaced by a web offset press.

Connaught Telegraph is the oldest paper in the county, indeed, one of the oldest in the whole country. Tom Courell, editor for the past fifteen years, delves into its background.

"The paper was launched on St Patrick's Day, 1828, as far as we know, and was started by a man called Lord Frederick Cavendish who lived here in Castlebar. He was a member of the gentry but at the same time had nationalist leanings. The paper has continued in production during those years and it's the proud boast of the firm here that we have never lost a week's production in all those years, taking us right up to today. From what we know initially, Lord Cavendish was the initial owner and subsequently it fell into the possession of a man called James Daly who was very much identified with the Land League. Subsequently it came into the ownership of the Gillespie family; that would have probably been about the turn of the century, and it has remained in the ownership of the Gillespie family since."

Tom Courell described the cosy atmosphere on the paper. "We are nearly a family, really, and that's the way the late Tom Gillespie, God be good to him, would like us to be, because Tommy himself when he was alive was a father figure to us all. He was a bachelor and he took a great interest not alone in his staff but in his staff's families and his influence alone seemed to bind us altogether."

The three Mayo papers are almost like one big family, competitive, but working amicably together when the occasion demands. P. J. Hennelly, the advertisement manager of the *Connaught Telegraph*, is a veteran of the business and a warm-hearted character revered up and down the country's weekly newspapers.

"Well, I am quite well known alright; I am chairman of the West of Ireland Newspapers' Association, where we have nine titles. We have meetings about every three months and we discuss all matters relating to the newspaper industry. We attend meetings regularly in Dublin of the Provincial Newspapers' Association of Ireland and of the advertising bureau of the weekly newspaper industry."

The "baby" of the Mayo papers, the *Mayo News*, has just celebrated its centenary. Sean Staunton, managing editor, explains its origins and how the paper rose phoenix-like from its own ashes.

"The paper was set up at either the end of 1892 or the beginning of 1893. Now we have more or less settled for the beginning of 1893, so we have recently celebrated our one hundredth birthday. The paper was set up by two Westport brothers, Pat and Willie Doris, who ran it for a lot of years and they encouraged not just the journalistic staff but the compositors as well to become involved in writing. Eventually it was bought again locally, the Durcan family were involved in it. Many years later, in 1946, *Inniu*, the Irish-language paper, and the *Mayo News* joined forces. Seven years ago the old technology had run its course and the paper got into some financial difficulties and for a while it looked as if it was going to close. But a local group of business people led by Joe Berry, who is one of the country's best-known printers and who actually started his own career in printing in the *Mayo News*, expressed an interest in it and he eventually bought the paper."

Since then, the paper has made great progress, producing editions of around forty pages every week, sometimes bigger. Martin Corry, the news editor, who has worked for the *Mayo News* for the past thirty-two years, remembers how in the old days the brother of Myles Na gCopaleen, Ciaran Ó Nuallain, was a regular visitor to the paper's offices in Westport.

"He certainly hadn't any humorous personality. He was a very serious character and very devoted to his work in connection with the *Inniu* newspaper, so certainly no jokes. No, he was friendly but serious and no jokes or quips or anything like that."

Sean Staunton says the paper encourages the use of Irish. "We do, because while I would not be totally fluent myself, I am very conscious of the previous connection with *Inniu* and the *Mayo News* for so many years. Parts of Achill are in the Gaeltacht. Tourmakeady is a Gaeltacht area, and we feel that as often as we can, we should be using the language in the paper. I would hope to develop that aspect more in the future."

By far the biggest problem for County Mayo is emigration, as Rita Devere Durcan explains. "We have an appalling emigration rate in the West of Ireland; it is to be deplored. The cream of our youth has had to emigrate because of the lack of job opportunities, and the *Western People* can be a real voice from home. Second and third generations who may have lost links would not get the amount of news from home were it not for the *Western People*."

Mayo's papers are as closely read abroad as they are at home. About 10 per cent of the *Western People*'s sales are made outside Ireland. "We send papers to the four corners of the earth. I have a list there in my briefcase of subscriptions and the complimentary copies and you would be amazed where the *Western People* goes to. You would be absolutely amazed", she concludes.

Knock Airport has made it much easier for exiles to go abroad and even more importantly to get home again. Tom Courell of the *Connaught Telegraph* describes the biggest West of Ireland news story in recent years.

"Knock Airport and its opening will probably stand out most in my mind, when the first planes arrived and flew off out to Rome. The late Monsignor James Horan was there in all his glory and maybe 30,000 people turned up just to see two or three planes arrive from, I think, either Shannon or Dublin, but they touched down on the airport there to pick up the passengers and take off again on an October day. That probably would have been one of the biggest news stories for us and probably one of the most exciting and memorable days. And then, of course, a very short time later we had the Monsignor himself. His remains were flown in from Lourdes where he died so suddenly. And that day the the crowds were there again but this time they were silent. Twenty to thirty thousand people crowded around the airport, along the perimeter fences, just watching this plane come in and his remains being taken from it. And there was such a contrast from the hype just a few short months before when he was there in all his glory, and banners waving and people excited and chanting and singing and a great sense of jubilation at the airport's success. How it had to fight the critics; then a couple of months later, people were out again but this time there was total silence, they were really numb."

To end where we started, John Waters, a well-known journalist with *The Irish Times*, himself from the West of Ireland, concludes by remembering perhaps the most vigorous and certainly the most famous journalist County Mayo has ever produced - John Healy.

"I couldn't believe this man. I had never seen anything like him before. Not only did he make me fascinated with him but he made me fascinated with where he came from and where I came from, because we had this great sense of place, this sense of the West of Ireland. We actually came from somewhere great, somewhere really significant."

Chapter 17

The Critics

• • •

CRITICISM HAS LONG HELD a prime place in Irish newspapers, but in the past ten years it has become more professional and informed, although an increased fear of libel has induced a certain caution which can be stultifying for readers. For much of the past century, theatre criticism has been the main sphere of critical activity, but with the arrival of other forms of entertainment, review writing has expanded in its scope. The advent of the cinema on a popular scale in the 1920s, TV in the 1960s and the compact disc in the 1980s all spawned new branches of this ancient craft. The development of music, including jazz and rock, has also been much enhanced. In recent years, brand-new review areas have opened up, especially restaurants and their gastronomic offerings. These often controversial critiques have become mandatory reading, making their authors stars in their own right.

Over a century ago, towards the end of the nineteenth century, theatre criticism was often in reality mere puffery, an exchange of editorial adulation for commercial approbation. Bram Stoker, creator of Dracula, was one of the first writers to improve the formula. In the 1870s, he became unpaid theatre critic for the Dublin *Evening Mail*, unrewarded financially because the paper sent its staff journalists to write its slight reviews and the then editor, Dr Henry Maunsell, had no wish to upset this little extra for his regular journalists. Stoker began writing well-constructed notices for nothing.

This century, an honourable tradition has been built upon, most notably at *The Irish Times*, where stalwarts of the craft have ranged from Seamus Kelly to Dr David Nowlan. Other papers, too, have long-serving astute theatre critics, like Des Rushe, drama critic on the *Irish Independent*, and

Mary MacGoris, also a critic on the *Irish Independent*. Another title in the group, the *Evening Herald*, had a remarkable theatre critic, John J. Finegan, who retired at the end of 1990 as drama critic of that paper, after forty-six years' service. He saw his first stage show in 1913, so he has been reporting on the Dublin theatre for two-thirds of this century, a remarkable record of longevity. His former colleague, Des Rushe, described him as kind, gentle, generous, loveable, awesomely knowledgeable, an institution of princely uniqueness. Out of his 2,145 pieces of theatre criticism for the *Evening Herald*, his most memorable first night was back in 1960, when Micheál MacLiammoir opened in *The Importance of Being Oscar*.

Yet theatre reviews, as with all other types of criticism, has its hazards for the reviewer. Ray Comiskey, who has written extensively about films for *The Irish Times* and who is now the paper's jazz reviewer, has a favourite theatre story from New York in the 1930s. "A famous critic of the *New York Post*, John Mason Brown, described the performance of an actor, whose name I think was Stone, as being the worst in contemporary theatre. Stone took a libel action against the critic, and while the case was pending, Stone appeared in another play, which Mason Brown was sent to review. Everyone in the know bought the paper the next day to see how he would handle this delicate situation, but Mason Brown contented himself with the observation that Mr Stone's performance was not up to his usual standard!"

The standard of reviewing in Irish daily newspapers has improved considerably. Ray Comiskey says: "I had the feeling sometimes that reviewers were picked for some areas of reviewing on the basis that if they were in the newsroom and could spell words of more than one syllable without having to hyphenate them, they were sent out to do the job."

Sometimes, professional writing expertise has to be augmented by elaborate precautions against libel. Restaurant reviews, one of the newest branches of the art for newspapers in Ireland, is also one of the most contentious. Helen Lucy Burke, who has written many combative pieces in her time for the *Sunday Tribune* and also for the *Irish Independent*, says she cannot go incognito. "I was unlucky to publish a book of short stories once, with my photograph on the back cover, and even though it was taken some years ago, it is recognisably me. All restaurants have my photograph, and some hotels, too."

She says that one of the favourite tricks of restaurateurs is to put lamb on the menu, which is disguised hogget, so when that happens she hoards the bones, measures and dates them.

"At least I will be able to produce them in court and say, 'Me lud, these are not the bones of a tiny little lamb, these are the bones of an adolescent sheep.'" On occasions when she has been reviewing hotels, her precautions are even more elaborate. "In a hotel bedroom, if it's ill lit, I would climb up and inspect the bulb, usually in that case it is a twenty watt. My travelling kit, when I am going to a hotel bedroom, consists of a pair of sheets, a pillowcase, a one hundred-watt bulb and of course my measuring tape. Everything is weighed and measured as far as I can do so. I measure the hotel room and the bed, and measure the hotel bathroom and the distance from the bathroom to the door. So if I say that the hotel bedroom is small, I can go to court and say I regard seven and a half feet by six feet as being a small bedroom."

Such caution and precaution was often unknown in the bad old days of newspaper criticism. When the noted poet, the dirty and irascible Paddy Kavanagh, sartorially scruffy, was film critic for the *Irish Press*, he often only stayed until half-way through a film, or on occasion never went to the performance at all. His reviews betrayed a vivid imagination. Other former critics were altogether more fastidious, like Charles Acton, for years music critic of *The Irish Times*, and the late John O'Donovan, who sat through concerts to prepare his reviews, always with a score sheet on his knee. Their approach was critical but gentlemanly and reservations about performances were taken in the spirit in which they were made. A similar approach has always prevailed with literary criticism.

Critics, like Terence de Vere White, formerly literary editor of *The Irish Times*, John Banville, present literary editor, Brian Fallon, chief critic of that paper, Dick Roche, formerly literary editor of the *Irish Independent*, and Ben Kiely, when he was literary editor of the *Irish Press* for so much of the 1950s and 1960s, have all been distinguished by a similarly fastidious intellectual approach to their work.

But some modern-day criticisms create a much more immediate reaction, as Helen Lucy Burke recalls. "You see these whitened faces looking out through the kitchen door. They are looking at something in their hand, which is obviously my photograph. They look again, greener and whiter." She has never been physically assaulted because of her writings, but it did get pretty physically steamy at a gathering of the

A galaxy of Dublin theatre critics at a presentation to Micheál MacLiammoir and Hilton Edwards in 1973, to mark the seventieth birthday of Hilton Edwards.

Front: Mary MacGoris (*Irish Independent*).

Second row, from left: Micheál MacLiammoir, the actor; Geraldine Neeson (*Cork Examiner* and *The Irish Times*) and Hilton Edwards.

Back row, from left: Dr David Nowlan (*The Irish Times*); Noeleen Dowling (then *Cork Examiner*, now *Evening Press*); John J. Finegan (*Evening Herald*); Des Rushe (*Irish Independent*); Seamus Kelly (*The Irish Times*); Gus Smith (*Sunday Independent*); John Boland (*Evening Press*); Patrick F. Byrne (*Evening Herald*); Desmond MacAvock (*The Irish Times*) and Emer O'Kelly (then *Sunday Press*, now RTE and *Sunday Independent*).

John J. Finegan (*right*), drama critic of the *Evening Herald*, makes a seventieth birthday presentation on behalf of the Drama Critics' Circle to Hilton Edwards, the actor. Also in the photograph from left: Micheál MacLiammoir, the actor, Geraldine Neeson (*Cork Examiner* and *The Irish Times*) and Noeleen Dowling (then *Cork Examiner*, now *Evening Press*).

Restaurants' Association.

"No one has ever thrown a punch at me in restaurant or theatre criticism. I had that in politics, when on two occasions people tried to murder me, literally, but they were a bit excited and there was an election on, so I forgave them afterwards." The most rugged experience she had was at an annual meeing of the Restaurants' Association of Ireland, held at Dromoland Castle in County Clare. Sandy O'Byrne from *The Irish Times*, Helen Lucy Burke and a critic from the US were on a panel for restaurateurs to question. "It was interesting to see them prowling around beforehand, like wolves hotting up for the kill, and I was the kill. They hurled abuse at me, they threw questions at me, they shouted and screamed."

However, she says that afterwards everyone had a great time; obviously, there were no hard feelings. But in recent years, disatisfaction on the part of a handful of restaurant owners has ended up with libel actions being taken against the newspapers and the reviewers in question. As a result of these actions, all newspapers are far more timid about including gutsy restaurant reviews. In the summer of 1992, Liz Ryan of the *Evening Herald* had food poisoning twice within a week while she was preparing to write reviews of the restaurants concerned.

"People think that you are having a wonderful time, swanning around restaurants and eating wonderful food, but in fact if you get a bad meal, like anyone else, you can be quite sick from it", she says. Liz Ryan planned to describe one of the restaurants where she had contracted food poisoning: "I wanted to write about this restaurant and the fact that I had been ill afterwards, but the editor decided no, saying that we were on very dangerous legal ground, even though the copy was factually correct." That incident brought to a head the question of continued restaurant reviews in the *Evening Herald* and since that date, the newspaper has published none.

Liz Ryan says that she would like to see a little more fighting back by the newspapers, "otherwise it will eventually reach a point where you won't be able to say anything about anyone or anything and no one will know what is going on. You will have censorship and self-imposed censorship at that."

If present trends continue, she believes, in five years' time newspapers may refrain from publishing many reviews, which would be bad news for the reading public and for the establishments concerned. However, the power and the press can be exaggerated. In some recent libel cases, restaurant owners claimed that bad reviews had put them out of business, but Ireland has never had a reviewer with the power of New York's Clive Barnes, able to close shows overnight with just a few damning comments. Relations between reviewers and their readers in Ireland have always been more intimate and rarely vitriolic.

Despite the dampening effect on reviews of the intimacy of the Dublin scene, and the Irish libel laws, the whole area of criticism and reviewing has built up into a substantial craft over the last one hundred years, forming one of the main components of many Irish newspapers.